52
Bible Talks
for
Fun and
Fruitfulness

David J. Schmeling

DISCIPLESHIP
PUBLICATIONS
INTERNATIONAL

Preface

Several years ago David Schmeling collected Bible talk outlines that he had used successfully, and his self-published book, *52 Bible Talks for Fun and Prophet,* was so well received that eventually DPI took over the printing, making it available to even more disciples.

After being out of print for a time, and after our churches went through a period when Bible talks were not used as often, DPI once again began to get requests for this book. This volume includes many of the outlines in Dave's original work, but also some material on hosting great Bible talks that was a part of a booklet done in the Boston church several years ago by Randy McKean and Roger Lamb. Our thanks to Toney Mulhollan for his insights into how to make this volume more useful, and for his efforts in reformatting the material to make it more attractive and readable.

The small Bible discussion group will always be a valuable tool for those seeking to win others to Christ. There is something special that happens when Christians invite their friends into their homes and then share personally how the Bible is affecting their lives. From the earliest days of our modern movement, thousands of people have been introduced to God and the Bible in these settings. The material in this book will prove helpful, especially to those who are young leaders, for having Bible discussions that are both fun and fruitful. May God bless you as you strive to point others to God.

Thomas Jones
Editor in Chief
Discipleship Publications International

Contents

Introduction

The Bible talks listed in this book are intended to:
- Be used like "soup starter" (a good base, but not a meal all by itself)
- Provide a basic outline for a Bible talk
- Give some good questions to kick off discussion
- Spark ideas on good Bible talk topics

The Bible talks listed in this book are *not* intended to:
- Eliminate preparation
- Replace the leader thinking about the needs of his/her people
- Substitute for personal Bible study on the part of the leader
- Provide personal examples

Please do:
- Add lots of personal examples and illustrations
- Consider the special needs of those in your group
- Tailor the questions to fit the members and visitors in your group
- Add to or modify the Bible talks to accommodate those in your group

Please do not:
- Pick out a Bible talk from this booklet five minutes before the meeting and try to lead a dynamic, exciting group Bible talk
- Use these Bible talks word for word
- Rely so heavily on these Bible talk outlines that you get stale
- Neglect learning how to put together your own Bible talk that will meet the specific needs of those in your group

Tips for Bible Talk Workers

Bible talk goals:
- To win people to Christ
- To edify the Christians–helping them know how to apply God's word
- Meet every week at the same place and time if possible
- Christians involved need to be regular in attendance and hard-working
- Christians need to be motivated by the love of Christ (2 Corinthians 5:14)
- Christians should be motivated by love for the lost (Matthew 9:36)

How to get people to the Bible talk:
- Work for the Bible Talk consistently–taking every opportunity to invite
- Don't pre-judge people before inviting them
- Start by making a list of all possible contacts
- Spend time with the people you want to invite
- Invite and get commitments ("maybes" don't usually come)
- Follow up and make sure they get there
- Plan to bring visitors with you–pick them up, walk with them to the location, etc.

What kind of atmosphere should there be before the Bible talk begins?
- It should not be quiet and tense or unfriendly
- It should be friendly and uplifting
- To be successful, you must be on time (even extra early)
- Introduce your visitors to others and introduce yourself to people you don't know
- Keep the conversations going until the leader says it's time to start

What is the disciple to do during the Bible talk?
- Affirm the Bible talk message from your personal life
- Comments should be on the subject and supportive
- Let the leader lead; do not change the direction of the Bible talk (no tangents)
- Think at all times, be alert and help your leader
- Do not condemn your old denominations, or denominations as a whole
- Do not make your comments too long–be concise
- Speak up when you talk–speak clearly
- If you are ignorant of a particular subject, don't feel compelled to comment
- Don't bring up a new comment when the leader is bringing the study to a close

How important is unity (team spirit) and how can it be developed?
- Unity is important–everyone must work together to reach people
- Make special efforts to encourage one another and to evangelize together
- Disciples should expect the best out of one another–like any team
- Pray daily for one another, as well as for the people being studied with and invited
- Members need to communicate with each other and with the leader about the people they are sharing with so that the leader is acquainted with needs of visitors

What to do after the Bible talk is over:
- Plan to stay a few minutes and talk with visitors
- Set up personal studies with those who are open
- Be sensitive to your visitors–get them home early so they'll want to come back
- Have refreshments after the study–so people can stay around and fellowship

Tips for a Great Bible Talk

Keep it simple
- People will generally remember only a few main points of the Bible talk
- You should be able to express the main point of the Bible talk in one simple sentence (If you can't, what are you expecting the people to remember?)

If possible, stick to just a few scriptures
- Pick a few passages, and dig into them
- Visitors will feel uncomfortable if they can't find scriptures
- You will spend more time in study and less time in searching for them
- People will be excited how much they can learn from just a few passages

Read the Scriptures in a powerful way
- Make the passage come alive in the reading and in your description of it
- Never make the Bible seem dull or boring
- If possible give a brief background on the scripture (who said it, when it was said, the circumstances) e.g. "Let's look at what Jesus had to say to the Pharisees on the subject of traditions."
- Always give a brief recap of the scripture in your own words (Some people get nervous during reading or have a hard time following the printed words on the page, so they are not able to concentrate on what is being read. A quick recap will bring everyone up to speed on what is happening in the passage.)
- Don't assume that everything in a passage is obvious (Remember you have spent hours studying this passage, the people in the group may be seeing it for the first time.)

Have fun
- Many passages and situations in the Bible are comical, have some fun when you talk about them. e.g.."Can you imagine what was going through the homeowners mind as those four guys were ripping through the roof to lower the paralytic down to Jesus?)
- Laugh with people and enjoy their comments
- Don't make the Bible talk "heavy" or "somber"

Teach with conviction
- Be convinced that what you are teaching is true and right, and that it will change the lives of your listeners (they need what you have to teach).
- Always leave people with a challenge. e.g. "The challenge from the study tonight is to get into the Bible to see what it takes to be a real disciple."

Make the Bible talk short
- Thirty to forty-five minutes maximum
- The mind cannot absorb what the bottom cannot endure
- If there are children, they will climb the walls if the study goes too long
- If the Bible talk is an all-night ordeal, visitors will not be back
- It is much better to leave people wishing the Bible talk had gone longer
- Leave a few points undiscussed to talk about in fellowship afterward

Make the openings fun
- Play a game of some kind (Name That Tune, Liar's Club, etc.)
- Show a video clip, play a song
- Read a newspaper article or a "Dear Abby" column
- Read some interesting facts, some articles from the web, etc.
- Go around and ask a non-threatening question of everyone (e.g.."If you could travel anywhere free, where would you go?")
- Use props (e.g. a mustard seed to illustrate faith)
- Be creative and fun
- Don't start the Bible talk with, "Let's all turn over to Isaiah..."

Set the atmosphere
- As the leader, you determine the atmosphere in the room
- Be sure the room is well-lit
- Teach the group members to be friendly
- Have great refreshments
- Occasionally have a potluck dinner before the Bible talk
- Make everyone feel at home
- Visitors are the focus of your conversation until they go home
- Avoid church lingo (e.g."D-time," "Discipler," "Devo," etc.)

Pay attention to detail
- Does everyone know when and where you are meeting?
- Does everyone have a ride?
- Be sure there are Bibles for anyone who has not brought one
- The members should be there fifteen minutes early to help clean, set up, give rides, buy refreshments, babysit kids for the host family, greet visitors as they arrive and whatever needs doing
- Clean your house or apartment (single brothers, are you paying attention?)

Pick six people to participate in a short ad-lib skit. Pick one reliable person to be the group's coordinator and brief him/her on what you are doing. Make paper headbands with the following wording:

I'm incompetent...treat me with contempt (give this one to the leader)
I'm funny...laugh at everything I say
I'm popular...try to be my friend
I'm smart...agree with me
I'm stupid...put me down
I'm a nobody...ignore me

Do not let the people see what their own headbands say. Have the coordinator lead this group in a five-minute skit in which they will plan a party for the Bible study. The discussion leader should be sure that each member is involved and that the rest of the people in the skit treat them according to what their headbands say. Stop the skit after five minutes.

Q: Ask those in the skit how they felt during the discussion.
• Labeled, confined, confused, trapped

Q: Have you ever been "labeled"? What is it like? Was it easy to break free?
• We all get labeled occasionally and put in a pigeonhole by others, but sometimes we get ourselves into a trap. We get trapped and we can't get out.

There are a number of traps that people get caught in:

1) Habit traps
Q: What are some?
• Smoking, swearing, overeating, drugs, alcohol, etc.

2) Character traps
Q: What are some?
• Selfishness, pride, insensitivity, etc.

3) Sin traps
Q: What are some?
• Fits of rage, pornography, immorality, etc.

Q: How do most people handle these traps?
• Ignore them, deny them, mask them
• Move from trap to trap–drugs, alcohol, sex, relationships
• Professional help (therapist) or self-help, self-improvement
• Distractions–shopping, eating, vacation, new things
• Blame shifting, bitterness, anger, frustration, rage
• Depression, despair, suicide

On your own, the prospects of breaking free are hopeless. On our own, mankind **does not** have the answers to free us from our traps. **I have good news!** God does have the answers, God is in the change business.

Lesson Scripture Let's look at a guy who had some real problems.
Mark 5:1-20 (Legion) Recap.

Q: What kind of problems did Legion have?
- No friends, violent, angry, weird, social misfit, rude, unfriendly, self-centered, self-destructive, lonely, out of control

It's easy to look down on Legion with all his problems, but people today aren't much different. Maybe some of you can relate to Legion: lonely, self-centered, rude, self-destructive, weird, social outcast, etc.

Q: Did Jesus do the right thing in healing Legion? Of course!

Q: Why? He needed healing. He needed to be set free.

Q: Do we need healing? Of course!

Q: Why does God want us to break free?
- He knows what makes us happy.

Q: What changed Legion?
- An encounter with Jesus (not a self-help book or a therapist)

Q: Do you see any evidence of change?
- Sitting there in his right mind! (v15)

Q: Was Legion excited about being set free? How do you know?
- This points out the difference between religion and relationship.

He didn't have to, but he wanted to go with Jesus.
He didn't have to, but he went to ten cities and told the good news!

Q: Are you religious, or do you have a relationship with Jesus?
- Do you grudgingly spend time with Jesus, or do you beg to be with him?
- Do you give the minimum possible, or do you give freely of your time and money?
- Do you just attend church, or are you sharing what God has done for you?

There is good news! Jesus can change you. You can break free.

The basis is not religion, but a relationship with Jesus Christ.

OPENER **Q: When you hear the word "authority," what is your first reaction?**

Q: What is the purpose of authority?
- Direct, protect, maintain order, promote unity, etc.

We "choose" to submit to authority.

Q: What happens when we choose not to submit?
- Penalty, conflict, chaos, etc.

Q: What are the benefits of submitting?
- Saved from penalties, fines, late charges
- Rewarded with raises, promotions, etc.

We all have the need to be under authority.
- It makes us happy, secure, confident.
- We have difficulty when others don't submit.
  e.g. A reckless or drunk driver, an unproductive co-worker
- We struggle submitting to those who don't themselves submit (i.e. the boss)
- Submitting to authority sets you free.

Jesus calls all people to submit to his authority.
Jesus was first submissive himself.
John 8:27-29
John 12:49-50
John 15:10

Note Jesus' submission: We are called to follow a humble, loving God!

Q: What keeps us from submitting?
- Pride, independence, selfishness
- A shallow understanding of Christ

Jesus was emphatic about obedience!

John 8:31-32. Need to hold to his teaching! It sets you free.

Note **Matthew 28:18-20.** Surely Jesus will be with you always!

 Conclusion Jesus is with you when you keep his commands and obey his authority.

Bible Talk #3

Born Again

OPENER Q: **What do you love about babies?**
- Most people get excited about new babies. (Have showers, announcements, etc.) They are sweet and cuddly and new. Jesus used children and babies on occasion to illustrate spiritual ideas.

Lesson Scripture John 3:1-12 (Nicodemus) Recap.

Q: **What can we tell about Nicodemus? What kind of person was he?**

Q: **What do you think he was after when he came to Jesus?**
- Probably wanted Jesus' stamp of approval
- Wanted to alleviate his nagging doubts

Q: **What do you think he expected Jesus to say?**
- You're doing great–just pray and tithe a little more and you'll be fine

Q: **What did Jesus say?**
- You must be born again.

Q: **What do you think Jesus meant by this?**
- You need to start all over again!

Several years ago the expression "born again" was commonly heard in the pop culture.

Q: **How would you describe a Christian who is not born again?**
- You can't! A Christian is someone who is already born again.

Q: **What is new about a baby after its birth (compared to before)?**
- New name, new family (relationships), new environment, new rules, new discipline, new food, new friends, and a whole new world!

Q: **What is new about someone who is born again?**
- New name (Christian)
- New family (church)
- New purpose (living for God)
- New goals
- New father (God)
- New behavior
- New everything!

There is a lot of confusion about the new birth.
The vast majority of people would claim to be born again.

14

Q: Why is there so much confusion about the new birth?
- Religious people make claims, but there is no evidence.
- People hear the claim, but don't see anything different about the person.

If you aren't sure you've been born again, you probably haven't been!

Q: What would you expect to see in someone who is born again?
- Radical life change in behavior, not just words
- He used to..., but now he....
- Is this the same person I used to know?

Q: Is being born again optional?
- No! v3–(unless...can't see the kingdom)
- v5–(unless...can't enter the kingdom)
- v7–(you must be born again)

Reread verses 5-7.
The new birth is not a physical event, it is spiritual.
It involves water and the spirit.
It's a heart change and a life change. It is exciting! It's a brand new start.

If you can't remember being born again, you haven't been.

If you think you've been born again, but there is no evidence, you haven't been.

Find out what the Bible says it takes to be born again. What did Jesus mean by the "water and the spirit"?

Get excited about a new beginning and a fresh start!

Are You Clean?

Activity On a sheet of paper, have everyone answer the following questions:

On average:
- How many showers or baths do you take a week?
- How many times a week do you brush your teeth?
- How many minutes per day do you spend getting ready for school/work?
- If you dropped a piece of bread on your kitchen floor, would you eat it?
- Would you ever use your spouse's/roommate's toothbrush?

Q: What do these questions have in common?
- Hygiene, cleanliness, taking care of yourself

Q: Are people in America into taking care of themselves? How so?
- Health, hygiene, physical fitness, fashion, style, trends, music, clothes, cars, hobbies, appearances, image, public relations

Q: What does it mean to be image conscious?

Q: Are most Americans image conscious? How so?
- Marketing, advertising hype are all based on image, appearance. Consider the hype, promotion over a can of beer, a car, a cigarette.
- Examples: Politicians, executives, stars and others hire agencies to do nothing but protect and promote their image.

You might think that Americans invented the idea of image consciousness, but there were some people who were into appearances a long time ago.

Lesson Scripture **Matthew 15:1-9** Recap.

Pharisees were concerned about cleanliness, appearances and image. In this passage Jesus talks about real cleanliness.

Q: How were the Pharisees being image conscious here?
- Honorary gifts to the temple gave an appearance of taking care of one's parents, but didn't.

Q: Why was Jesus so upset with them?
- They had the appearance of being loving and devoted, but they weren't.
- They were really selfish and greedy.

In love, Jesus laid out the truth. He never minced words, but told people the truth and applied it to their situations.

Lesson Scripture **Matthew 23:1-7, 23-28** Recap.

Jesus addressed religious leaders who talk a good game, but do not live up to God's standard.

Q: Why was Jesus so hard on them?
- They were concerned about how they looked, not with being righteous.
- They were blinded by religion and hypocritical attitudes.
- They were focused on the external appearance, not true righteousness.
- They exchanged knowing the answers for living the answers.

Q: What was Jesus concerned about?
- The heart...the inside of the cup!

Q: Why was he so concerned about the heart?
- Jesus wants us to be in love with God.
- He wants us to have a **want to** attitude, not a **have to** attitude.

Example: How would you like to be married to someone who didn't want to be married to you? You might do all the right things, but if you weren't in love...

The challenge for us is to not be like the Pharisees: They cleaned the outside of the cup, but left the inside dirty.

Q: How do we show more concern for the outside of the cup than the inside?
- Show up for church or a Bible study, but not really want to be there
- Talk spiritual talk around Christians, but act differently in the world
- Act like we have no sin, hide our flaws, cover our faults
- Put on a religious front, but hate it when we are alone

Proverbs 4:23 ("Above all else, guard your heart, for it is the wellspring of life.") Your heart is so important. It is who you are.

Q: Why aren't we more concerned about the inside of the cup?
- It's harder, it takes more work, more persistence
- It isn't as glamorous and flashy
- It isn't as obvious–it's easy to dress nice, talk nice, act spiritual, but very hard to be spiritual

Each one of us:
- Needs to start cleaning the inside of the dish
- Needs to spend less energy looking good, and more energy being good.
- Needs to worry more about what God thinks of us than what people think of us
- Needs to live the life of a disciple and not play at religion

 Start making the effort to be right with God, and not to play at Christianity. Grab someone who is spiritual and get some help. Start reading/studying the Bible to see how to clean the inside and the outside of the dish.

What Makes You Happy?

Q: **What makes you happy?**

Q: **What used to make you happy?**

Q: **What would make you happy if you could have it now?**

 Examine King Solomon's search for happiness and fulfillment, and apply it to our search today.

1. Learning. **Ecclesiastes 1:12-13, 16**

Q: **Share a time when you felt learning a new business or trade was the answer to happiness.**

Q: **What was the result?**

Ecclesiastes 1:17-18 The more you know, the more you see you don't know.

2. Luxury. **Ecclesiastes 2:4-10**

Q: **How do you feel the day you buy something new?**

Q: **How do you feel the day later? A week? A month? A year?**
- Time for a different one or a new one
- A new car may warm your heart but it won't change it
- Chasing after the wind (v11)

3. Liquor. **Ecclesiastes 2:3**

Q: **What does one glass of wine do for you?**
- Warms your insides, enhances some food

Q: **What does too much do?**
- Turns Joe Cool into Joe Cruel or Joe Fool or Joe Crazy or Joe Lazy
- It destroys lives and relationships
- There are 15 million known alcoholics in the U.S.

Proverbs 23:29-32

4. Lust. **Ecclesiastes 2:8-10, 1 Kings 11:3** (700 wives, 300 in his harem)

Q: **What does lust do to a person? To a marriage?**
- Pornography, rape, murder, child molesting, etc.

5. Lord. **Ecclesiastes 12:13-14**

 The only true and lasting fulfillment comes through loving God and obeying his commands.

Healing the Hurts of the Past

OPENER

Q: Have you ever been stopped by a policeman, but not been ticketed?

Q: How did it feel?

Q: Cite other examples in which you should have been in trouble, but got off.
- It feels good to escape the penalty!
- The need in our marriages and in our relationships is to make others feel this way–in other words to forgive them.

Q: What are some obstacles to forgiving others?
- Desire for revenge
- Desire for satisfaction (apology)
- Reluctance to face the issue

Q: Why do we need to forgive? Discuss.

Let's see what the Bible has to say about this topic:

Matthew 6:14-15	To receive God's forgiveness
Colossians 3:13	To imitate the Lord
Ephesians 4:32	Because it is a command
Hebrews 12:14-15	To avoid bitterness

Q: What is typically required of a person in order for us to forgive them?
- An apology, evidence of repentance

Luke 23:34 Jesus on the cross.

Q: What did Jesus require? Nothing

Luke 17:3-4	If a person repents, you must forgive them.
Luke 17:5	Disciples thought it would take more faith.
Luke 17:6	Jesus said (in effect,) to use the faith you have.

We can forgive all by ourselves! It is an isue of your heart–no one else's.

Q: How do you feel when you really forgive someone?
- Free, like a burden has been lifted
- Released, relieved
- Healed and forgiven
- Clear conscience
- Free from bitterness

Conclusion

1. Healing the hurts of the past is available now! We can begin the healing process now (all alone if need be).
2. We are commanded by God to forgive from the heart.
3. There are great benefits to relationships when we forgive.

Bible Talk #7

Healing at the Pool

 OPENER Discuss the current emphasis on health: jogging, health clubs, food, etc.

Q: What are you doing to stay in shape and stay healthy?

 Lesson Scripture **John 5:1-15** Recap.
(Use the physical to illustrate the spiritual.)

Q: What does "disabled" mean?

Q: "Blind," why do we use that term?

Q: What causes spiritual blindness?
- We prefer the darkness over the light.

Q: "Lame," why do we use that term?

Q: How can we be spiritually lame?
- We can become weak, just limping along, because we aren't relying on the Word to strengthen us.

Q: "Paralyzed," why do we use that term?

Q: What causes spiritual paralysis?
- We allow sin and guilt to paralyze us, rather than getting open and getting help so that we can become strong and healthy spiritually.

Q: What is your "disability"?

" I am trying..." is not good enough. (v7)

Q: What excuses have you used?
- We prefer the darkness over the light.

 Challenge Do you want to get well? The solution is the same today as then...Jesus!

Bible Talk #8

Controversy

 OPENER Name a controversial topic!
- Abortion, condoms in the schools, gun control, genetic engineering, euthanasia, etc.

Q: What makes something controversial? Emotional involvement

Q: Do you like to be involved in controversy? Why? Why not?

There are some things that people don't mind being controversial about, but most people certainly don't want their religion or their church to be involved in controversy. Most churches and most religious people are "nice," and don't want to offend or cause trouble. In our society, that is the way religion is supposed to be.

Let's look at the Bible and see if it can shed some light on this subject.

 Lesson Scripture **The Controversial Jesus**

John 7:25-44 Recap.

Q: Do you see anything controversial about Jesus?
- Questioning, debate (v25)
- Some believed, some wanted to arrest him (vv30-32)
- The people were divided (vv41-44)

Q: What caused the controversy?
- Jealousy (vv31-32)
- Ignorance, didn't have all the facts (vv41-43)
- Speculation and ignorance (v35)
- Jesus was different, didn't agree with the popular teaching of the day

Q: How did people react to the controversy?
- vv25-26 bewildered; v25 wanted to kill him; v31 some believed
- v32 competitive; vv30, 44 anger/malice/hate; v40 he is a prophet
- v41 he is the Christ; v42 he is an imposter

Jesus caused quite a stir among the people. He divided people. He caused discussion, debate, questioning of the normal way of thinking. Some of Jesus' critics called him mad, deceived and a demon. Some even questioned his parentage and his upbringing.

Q: Was there anything controversial about Jesus' birth? Yes!

Q: Was there anything controversial about his death?
- Yes! Jesus wasn't just a nice guy, or a sweet religious man. From birth to resurrection, Jesus was controversial. Jesus caused controversy at every turn.

The Controversial Church

Lesson Scripture Acts 5:1-14 (Ananias and Sapphira) Recap.

Q: What do you think was being discussed in Jerusalem the next day?

Q: How do you think the story was handled in the *Jerusalem Gazette*?
- "Couple struck dead in local church for not giving enough!!"

Q: How do you think people in the church reacted?

Q: Some probably left, what do you think they said?

Q: Was there any controversy in how the early church began?

Q: Was the spread of the early church controversial?

Q: Who persecuted the early church? Religious people!

Q: Why did they persecute the early church?
- It was having an impact on people, taking away their followers! From its beginning, the early church was controversial. Just read Acts. It wasn't the "nice" church on the corner with the pretty steeple. It stirred things up, it confronted sin, it challenged religious hypocrisy.

What about you and the church you attend?

Q: What is controversial about a true disciple of Jesus Christ?
- Commitment, relationships, purity, humility, service, righteousness

Q: If you were as committed as the Bible teaches, what would people say?

Q: If you were as pure as the Bible teaches, what would people say?
- If you are trying to be like Jesus, you will be controversial.

Q: What is controversial about a church imitating the church of the Bible?
- Unity, giving, evangelism, submission, love, commitment

Q: If a church were as unified as the Bible teaches, what would people say?
- If your church is imitating the early church, it will be controversial.

Some of us have bought the world's view of Christianity.
Don't make waves, blend in, be nice, accept everyone, don't upset anyone. Some churches have bought into the world's view of church: nice programs, attractive places of worship, nice people, no guidelines, no absolutes, no controversy.

Does your life stir controversy? Does your church cause controversy?

Follow Jesus and you will be controversial!

The Cost of Discipleship

 ER Q: **Which classes in college or high school stand out in your memory? Why?**

Q: **What kind of teachers did you enjoy or respect the most? Least?**
- Typically we like and respect the teachers who demand a lot from us.

Jesus taught some challenging and demanding things. For example, he said: "Love the Lord your God with all of your heart, mind and strength" and "Go and make disciples of all nations..."

Jesus always asked for and expected the best from people, never second best, never mediocrity. Let's look at another challenging teaching of Jesus.

Lesson Scripture **Luke 14:25-33** Read and recap.

Q: **Who was following Jesus?**
- Large crowds–Jesus was beginning a ministry, trying to gain followers, support

Q: **If you were in his position, and had gathered a large crowd, what might you say?**
- Some nice things, nothing controversial, nothing too hard considering this is the first time many heard
- Something positive and encouraging

Q: **What does Jesus do?**
- He thins the crowds! He makes great demands on their lives.

Q: **What were some of the reasons people were following Jesus?**
- To be healed, to see all the strange happenings, to be entertained
- To find out what Jesus was all about, if he really was the Messiah

Jesus wasn't after large numbers! He was after true followers!

Q: **What does Jesus mean in verse 26?**
- He wants first place in our lives. It is a reordering of relationships.

Q: **How do you know if someone loves Jesus more than a wife, husband, children or self?**
- They obey God's will first, doing what he wants and not what they want. Notice that if you won't do this, Jesus doesn't say you will be a weak disciple or a growing disciple. No, Jesus says you can't even be a disciple!

Q: **Is this challenging to anyone?**

Q: **What does it mean in verse 27 to pick up your cross and follow Jesus?**

Q: What was a cross used for?
- Torture, suffering, pain and persecution, execution

We must be willing to suffer for Jesus, to be uncomfortable, to be persecuted, to go through some rough trials and difficulty because of Jesus.

Q: Is this challenging to anyone?
- Jesus is challenging and demanding, but incredibly honest. He is up front about what is required to follow him, not like some salesmen or televangelists.

Read vv28-30. (Counting the cost)

Q: What does this story mean?
- We must sit down and count the cost of following Jesus.

Q: Have you ever made an emotional decision? When?
- Bought a new car on a whim, got married on a whim, etc.

Q: What happens when the going gets rough, or it isn't what you expected?
- People bail out on their payments, on contracts, on their marriages and on God if they don't feel like continuing. Jesus said sit down and count the cost, think about it and decide if you are willing to do it.

Read vv31-32. (The cost of **not** being a disciple) Recap.
Jesus is the strong king, you are the weak king.

Q: Who sets the terms? Jesus

Q: What if you don't like the terms? You get wiped out!

Think about these questions for a moment:
- Will you be a better spouse if you are a disciple? Or not a disciple?
- Will you be a better parent if you are a disciple? Or not a disciple?
- Will you stand a better chance of going to heaven if you are a disciple?

It's smart to be a disciple. Everything goes better and you go to heaven!
It's absurd to reject Jesus' terms. You're worse off, and when you die, you go to hell.

Read v33. Example: Jesus holds out a tray in his hand and says let's have it all: your job, house, car, spouse, kids, hobbies, free time, sports, personality, sin, relationships, dreams, goals, ambitions, career, education and yourself.

You must give it all to Jesus, or you can't be a disciple.

Q: Why would anyone voluntarily give up everything?
- Only if they love God, fully trust him, and are convinced it is worth it!

Challenge

If you want to be a disciple, you must have a disciple's commitment. If you don't have a disciple's commitment, you aren't following Jesus.

If you are not sure if you want to be a disciple, then:
1) You don't know Jesus well enough yet.
2) You don't fully understand what you are being offered.

Bible Talk #10 | Light and Darkness

 OPENER Start the study with the lights on.
Turn out the lights (curtains drawn), and ask someone to read.
Turn on the lights and start the study.

Q: Discuss how people feel about being in darkness.
- Can't see
- Easily run into things, not confident going in any direction
- Can hurt oneself
- Magnifies all our fears

Q: Discuss how people feel about being in the light.
- Everything is in sight
- Can see obstacles
- Can move ahead without fear of being hurt

Read **1 Peter 2:9-10.**
God compares being a Christian to being in the light and out of the darkness.

Q: What do people do when they have the light?
- Declare the praises of God, become people of God, receive mercy

Read **1 John 1:5-10.**
Q: How do we know if we are walking in the darkness or the light?
- If we claim we don't sin, we're in darkness.
- If we live in unrepentant sin, we're in darkness.
- If we confess our sins and repent of them, we're in the light.
- If we have fellowship with the son, we're in the light.

Read **1 John 2:3-6.**
Q: How does obedience to God's word keep us in the light?
- We know that we have come to know him if we obey his commands.
- If we claim to live in him, we will walk as Jesus did.

Read **2 Timothy 3:1-5.**
Q: We can have a form of godliness (be religious), but not be in the light.
- Discuss each sin and how they keep us in darkness and fear.

Read **Titus 2:11-14.**
Q: What is the attitude of someone walking in the light?
- Teaches us to say no to ungodliness and worldly passions
- Live self-controlled, upright and godly lives
- Eager to do what is good

 Challenge Are we living in the light or darkness? Are we willing to do whatever it takes to get out of the darkness and into the light?

Jehoiakim Burns the Scrolls

Bible Talk #11

OPENER Q: **Have you ever read something in the Bible you wish you could take out?**
  • Tonight is your chance! Share the story of Thomas Jefferson, who actually took his Bible and cut out all the passages that referred to miracles because he didn't believe they were possible.

Lesson Scripture Read **Jeremiah 36:1-26.** (Jehoiakim and the scrolls)

Activity Pass out slips of paper and let people write down what they would delete from the Bible (include references if possible).

Collect papers and have a ten-minute break.

During the break, make up a revised version of the Bible based on the papers collected.

Read **Jeremiah 36:28-32.**

Q: **Did ignoring God's word make it go away?**

Q: **What is the consequence of deleting things from God's word?**

Q: **Do we have the right to play games with God's word?**

Q: **How do people practically exhibit this attitude toward the Bible?**
  • Arbitrarily decide what is applicable and not applicable for today
  • Decide what is outmoded and no longer fits with today's world
  • Don't treat God's word with seriousness

Read **1 Peter 1:24-25.**
"All men are like grass, and all their glory is like the flowers of the field; the grass withers and the flowers fall, but the word of the Lord stands forever."

Masks

Have a discussion about masks. What masks do people like at Halloween? Perhaps discuss the movie, *The Mask,* and how the mask transforms Jim Carey into a totally different person, etc.

People wear masks more than just at Halloween. Discuss some of the different masks that people wear:

Mask of coolness–nothing ruffles them
Mask of superiority–can't top them in anything
Mask of religion–communicates perfection
Mask of inferiority–false humility
Mask of the Joke–never gets deep or serious
Mask of Macho–a continual sense of bravado
Mask of niceness–covering a heart of bitterness
Mask of respectability–never does anything "improper"
Mask of the intellectual–never stoops to mundane thoughts
Mask of the athlete/playboy

Q: Why do people wear masks?
- To cover up who they really are
- Fear of being rejected
- To feel superior over others

Q: According to the Bible, why do people cover up?
- Fear of "evil" deeds being exposed. John 3:19-21.

Lesson Scripture

Read **Mark 7:20-23.** Define what the Bible calls "sin."

Q: What is the commonality in this list of sins?
- All are evil, come from the inside and make us unclean. These are what people really want to hide. These are what people cover up.

Solution
1) **John 3:21**–Live by truth.

2) **2 Corinthians 5:17**–In Christ we are a new creation, and we're free to take off the masks and be transparent.

3) **2 Corinthians 3:12-18**–"But whenever anyone turns to the Lord, the veil is taken away." (v16) It is only in Christ that we can be honest and be real. The veil is removed from our faces and we have the opportunity to reflect the Lord's glory instead of hiding who we really are inside.

Make a decision tonight to remove the masks in your life. Be transparent, and let God clean the inside. Then we won't need to wear masks!

Convince the Skeptic

 To start the study, tell the group that you are going to be doing some role playing.

Tell the group that you want to become a Christian, but you have some questions you need to have answered.

It is their job to convince you, from the Scriptures, that you need to become a Christian tonight.

Let your Christians know a week ahead of time about the study you are going to do so they can be prepared to answer your objections.

Some typical questions or objections:
- I don't think I can put God before some relationships
- I'm not good enough to be a Christian
- Having too much fun being a sinner
- I don't know if I can be that committed
- Some personal examples might spur me on
- Can't I put it off until the end of the year, or the semester, etc?
- Is there really a hell and will God actually punish people?
- I don't "feel" like it's the right time
- I was raised in a Christian home, isn't that enough?
- I'm as good as most Christians I've seen

You want the visitors to know that the Bible deals with any and all objections we can come up with that would stop them from becoming disciples.

 Conclude with **Acts 22:16**: "And now what are you waiting for? Get up, be baptized and wash your sins away, calling on his name."

Lesson Scripture

What a Blind Man Saw

Read **John 9:1-34.** This study is centered around the five different types of characters in this passage and their responses to Jesus.

1. **John 9:1-7.** The response of Jesus' disciples:

Q: How did the disciples react to the blind man's situation?
- Looked for someone to blame

Q: What hinders us from seeing God's purposes in our lives?
- Lack of faith, sin, inadequate understanding of God, etc.

2. **John 9:8-12.** The blind man's neighbors:

Q: What kind of neighbors were these, and how did they relate to him?
- Not sure it was their neighbor, obviously a superficial relationship

Q: How did they react to the healing of the blind man?
- Healing so miraculous they had their doubts if it was the same man

3. **John 9:13-34.** The religious leaders:

Q: How did the Pharisees react and why did they feel threatened?
- They were divided and argued over points of theology instead of a changed life

Q: How did tradition blind them to the truth?
- If they accepted it, it would call them to follow Jesus and leave their tradition

Q: How do we exhibit the same attitudes as the Pharisees?
- We refuse to question our traditions, we refuse to change, and instead of thinking, we insult or attack the truth

4. **John 9:18-23.** The blind man's parents:

Q: What kind of relationship did the parents have with their son?
- They must have been ashamed, they let him beg on the streets

Q: What else kept them from acknowledging this miracle?
- Peer pressure–They were afraid of being put out of the synagogue

Q: How does peer pressure keep us from becoming Christians?
- Afraid of what others will think, how it will affect us on the job, promotions, acceptance of family, friends, etc.

5. **John 9:7, 35-41.** The blind man:

Q: What kinds of characteristics stand out about this man?
- Simple obedience
- Unafraid of what others thought, even his own parents
- Willing to take a stand and speak out

Challenge

Which of these five types of characters most reflect your life?

What will it take for you to have the same faith and attitude as the blind man?

Rich Toward God

 Have each person share a slogan, then have others in the group guess the product or company. Examples:

"Just do it!"–Nike
"It just taste better"–Burger King
"Don't leave home without it"–American Express Card
"You never looked so good"–Avon
"When you care enough to send the very best"–Hallmark

Q: What do advertising agencies appeal to in their ads and slogans?
• Security, fun, self-worth, image, pleasure, acceptance, sex, etc.

Advertisers create a perceived need, and then they fill it with their product.

Q: What hinders us from seeing God's purposes in our lives?
• Lack of faith, sin, inadequate understanding of God, etc

Q. What is the American dream?
• House, nice car, college education, wife, kids, MBA, fat bank account, boat, DVD player, entertainment centers, looking sharp, dressing nice, etc.

Q: How well has the American dream served America? Why?

 Let's look at some input Jesus had about wealth and riches.

Lesson Scripture Luke 12:13-21 (Rich fool) Recap.

Q: Why did Jesus say, "watch out?"
• We need to, there is danger! Greed sneaks up on us.

Q: What is the danger? What is "all kinds of greed"?
• Money, power, materialism, selfishness, chasing riches, jealousy, envy

Q: What would most people's opinion be about this man?
• Successful, hard-working, ambitious, wealthy, deserved a break

Q: What did Jesus say about this man?
• Called him a fool!

Q: Why did Jesus call him a fool?
• He missed the most important things of life–he missed the big picture.
• He was selfish and was storing things up for himself. It cost him his life.
• Jesus says this will happen to anyone who is not rich toward God!

 Are we rich toward ourselves or are we rich toward God? If your checkbook and your time schedule were looked at, what would they say you are rich toward?

Bible Talk #16

Give Thanks to God

 Q: What are some ways that you can see selfishness in young children?
- Unwillingness to share toys, etc.

Q: What are some ways that you see selfishness in adults?
- Unwillingness to share their expensive toys, etc.

Q. What are some examples of self-focus in our society?
- *Self* magazine, walkmans, self-indulgence, etc.

 Read **Luke 17:11-19.** Recap.

Q: What would it be like to be a leper?
- Humiliating, lived outside of town in segregated communities, no source of income other than begging, sores, deterioration of health, ostracized

Q: How do you think they felt?

Q: Have you ever felt that way? When?

Jesus saw them and said, " 'Go show yourselves to the priests.' And as they went, they were cleansed." (v14) Of the ten who were healed, only one came back to thank Jesus, and he was a Samaritan.

Q: What are some possible reasons the others didn't return to thank Jesus?
- Too busy
- It wasn't convenient
- They would thank him later
- Ignorant of the magnitude of what had been done for them
- Figured Jesus would know that they were thankful.
- "I obeyed, I did as Jesus commanded. Isn't that enough?"

Q: Would you say that these people believed in Jesus? Why?
- Called Jesus master and obeyed him

Q: How do you think Jesus felt about the nine ungrateful lepers?
- Hurt, disappointed, sad and let down

Q: How are we like the nine?
- Take God and his miracles in our lives for granted
- Don't give thanks, or give him credit for what we have
- Don't talk to God and express our thanks
- Do the bare minimum, just enough to get by
- Get lazy and lose our focus

Reread vv15-16.

31

Q: What do you see about the Samaritan leper?
- Praised God in a loud voice and was not concerned with what people thought
- He was humble, fell at Jesus' feet
- His faith made him well

Q: How do we need to imitate the Samaritan leper?
- Remember what God has done for us
- Obey God's commands
- Give God the praise and credit he deserves

Q: What stops us?
- Too busy
- It wasn't convenient
- God knows my heart
- "I don't need to be that radical in my love for God"
- There is no shortage of excuses we can give for not being grateful

All were physcially healed , but only one received spiritual healing.

Ingratitude hurts God. Recognize where your blessings come from.

Be a thankful person–to God, to parents, to spouse, to friends, to everyone who has made a difference in your life.

Bible Talk #17

Hot or Cold?

OPENER Go around the room and introduce yourselves. Answer the following question:

Q: What is your favorite cold food? And favorite hot food?

Q: What foods are gross at room temperature?
* Milk, soups, casserole, pizza, beer, etc.

We use "hot" and "cold" to describe many things besides food and weather.

Q: What expressions do we use with the adjectives "hot" or "cold," and what do the expressions mean?
* The entertainment was hot! (It was great!)
* He was pretty cold. (He was very unfriendly.)
* The basketball play was cold. (Couldn't hit any shots)
* Get hot! (Get going. Make something happen. Start working hard!)

The Bible has used the words "hot" and "cold" to describe our relationship with God. "Hot" means it is exciting, dynamic, growing and fun. "Cold" means it is stale, dead and lifeless.

Let's look at a section of the Bible that talks about a group of people and what their walk with God was like.

Lesson Scripture Revelation 3:14-22 (Letter to the church in Laodicea) Recap.

Q: The people there had two major problems. What were they?
* Lukewarm
* Out of touch with their own spiritual condition

Q: What does it mean to be lukewarm?
* Half-hearted, indifferent, mediocre, getting by, minimum requirement

Q: Have you ever done something in a lukewarm way? When?

Q: Have you ever had someone do something for you in a lukewarm way?

Q: How would you like your doctor to treat you in a lukewarm way?

Q: How would you like a lukewarm relationship with your spouse?
* It would make you sick!

Look at v16–It means vomit! Being lukewarm makes God want to throw up!

Either love God and serve him like you said you would, or stop pretendin

Reread v17a.

Q: What do you notice about these people?
- They think everything is going great, when they are really out of touch

Q: What kind of attitude is this, "I don't need a thing"?
- Prideful, arrogant, boastful, stupid

Q: What are the people really like?
- Wretched, pitiful, poor, blind and naked

Q: If you were to walk into this group of people, what would they be like?
- Rich, well-dressed, polite, friendly, well-groomed, educated
- Would seem to have it together, seem like they don't need a thing

This always reminds me of religious America: nice, educated, polite, but not doing anything significant. Their deeds were neither hot nor cold. (v15)

Q: What do you think God would say is a "hot" deed?
- Making a disciple (helping someone become a Christian)
- Sacrificing some time to help someone in need
- Sacrificing some money to see the gospel spread
- Dealing with your sin in a radical way, making a radical change
- Challenging sin in someone else's life, confronting sin

Q: What have you done lately that God would say is "hot"?

The sad part is that these people were so out of touch.

Q: How did these people end up so oblivious to their condition?
- Didn't read God's word and didn't pray
- Didn't get input from godly men and women
- Were independent, self-reliant
- Used themselves as the standard, not God

Q: Is it possible that some of us are in a similar situation?
- Of course, in fact you can bank on it

- Recognize if you are lukewarm and decide to be hot for God.
- Stay in God's word and study it as the standard.
- Get some godly men and women in your life who will tell you the truth.
- Listen and be receptive to what they say.

Bible Talk #18

Humility and Submission

 OPENER Look at two or three television commercials with the entire group. Analyze what techniques were used to sell the product and why.

Advertising is defined as: "To call public attention by emphasizing desirable qualities so as to arouse a desire to buy or patronize."

 Lesson Scripture **Philippians 2:1-8** Recap.

Q: If you were an advertising account executive and you wanted to get the account with God the Father to market the coming of Jesus Christ on earth, how would you package and sell the following aspects of his life?

1. His birth
   * Baby shower, nice hospital, announcements, gifts, flowers, nice nursery, best medical care, best clothes, great name

2. His profession
   * Politician, successful businessman, great education

3. His personal attributes
   * Rich and famous family (nobility), good looks, etc.

4. Ministry
   * Choose a time with modern communication and transportation

5. Entourage (disciples)
   * A rich man, a theologian, four strong bodyguards, two charismatic and powerful speakers, a popular personality, a politician with clout, an educated man, a strategist, etc.

6. His finale (exit)
   * Trumpets, sky opening up, fireworks, blazing ride up to heaven
   * (No death–too depressing)

Q: How did Jesus actually do it?
   * Everything Jesus did was full of humility–from birth to death.

In America, we take pride in being free and independent. (e.g. pilgrims, labor unions, democracy, constitution, Bill of Rights, etc.). Yet there is a danger in the motivation behind these concepts.

1 Peter 2:16 says not to use your freedom as an excuse to sin.

Q: How do we do that?
   * Use our "rights" to sue people, go on strike, etc. for petty, selfish reasons, etc.

Let's discuss some areas in which humility is difficult to practice.

1. Self
   Paul said, "I am the worst of sinners." **(1 Timothy 1:15)** Paul was very humble, open and honest about himself to others and before God.

Q: How are we not humble before God?
- Don't admit we need God
- Don't obey God's commands (we think we know a better way)
- Not admitting our sins
- Put our feelings before God's word
  We need to be humble before God!

2. Family
   Guidelines are given for the whole family. **(Colossians 3:18-21)**
   It isn't just the kids! It's dad and mom! Kids will imitate them.

Q: How are we not humble at home?
- Don't admit we're wrong with our spouse and kids
- Don't listen to each other's feelings
- Don't put the others' needs first
  We need to be humble at home to experience the kind of family God desires!

3. Occupation
   We need to serve our employer as though he were Jesus. **(Ephesians 6:7-8)**

Q: If you are humble at work, what will others think?
- Kissing up, trying to win points
- No backbone, a "yes" man, not an independent thinker
- Trying to work too hard and make others look bad
  We need to be humble and submissive at work!

4. At Church
   Obey your leaders **(Hebrews 13:17)**

Q: Is this seen in most churches today? Why? Why not?
- People go to the church of their choice or whim instead of the church God desires
- People think church is a democracy similar to the government
- People are used to getting their way if they are loud enough
- People are used to being waited on and served by leaders (it's their job, they get paid to serve, etc.)

 There is always a good reason (excuse) not to be humble. Read **Philippians 2:9-11.** God exalted Jesus because of his humility. God's ways are so contrary to our thinking.

"God opposes the proud but gives grace to the humble." **(James 4:6)**

Does your life demonstrate humilty and submission, or arrogance and pride?

A Fishing Expedition

OPENER **Q: Have you ever been in a jam and made a promise to God?**
- "God, if you get me out of this jam, I'll..."

Lesson Scripture Let's look at a story of someone who got in a real jam.

Jonah 1-3 Recap.

1. God has given us direction in our lives; a mission to accomplish.

Q: What did God give Jonah to do?
- Go preach to Ninevah.

Q: What job has God given us to do?
- Go make disciples. (**Matthew 28:18-20**)

Q: Why did God send Jonah to Ninevah?
- The people needed God; they were lost.

Q: Why does God want us to make disciples?
- People need God and are lost without a relationship with him.

Think for a minute about the people you know who need God; in their marriages, in the raising of their children, in their relationships, in their character.

The word of the Lord came to Jonah. (**Jonah 1:1**)

Q: How does the word of the Lord come to us?
- God's word–the Bible
- Spiritual people
- Conscience guided by the Holy Spirit

2. How are you responding to God's direction for you?

Q: What do you think of Jonah's effort to run away from God?

Q: How are we like Jonah?
- God's laws apply, whether or not we read them or understand them!

Q: God could have found anyone to go to Ninevah, but what was the real issue?
- Lordship, is God our God? Is Jesus going to be our Lord?

God can send someone else to your friends, family and neighbors, but the same issue stands–Is Jesus Lord? Are you going to obey his direction or not?

Q: How do you see God working in Jonah's life?
- The storm and the fish were sent directly by God.

When you obey God, God works with you and through you.

When you disobey God, you suffer bad consequences and you may even find God actually opposing you.

3. The most hopeless people can come to God.

Q: What do you know about the people of Ninevah?
- Separated from God, pagan, ignorant

Read **Jonah 3:1-4.**
Q: What does it seem Jonah was thinking?
- Excited, totally repentant, totally faithful–perhaps skeptical, wondering, doubting if the people of Ninevah would respond to God

Read **Jonah 3:5-10.**
Q: How did the people of Ninevah respond?
- The King of Ninevah repented. (v6)
- Even the cattle were clothed with sackcloth (a sign of humility). What an incredible response!

There are some valuable lessons here:
1. The most hopeless people can respond to God (aren't we all hopeless?).
2. The power is not in the messenger, but in the power of God and his message.
3. You don't have to be slick, polished, eloquent, wise, a great speaker, or even totally faithful or mature–just obedient!

When Moses parted the Red Sea, God did it.
When Joshua brought down the walls of Jericho, God did it.
When Peter walked on water, God did it.
These people could never have done it on their own power, and neither can we.
Only when we obey does God give the power to accomplish it.

1. God has given us some direction and a mission to do.
2. We need to be obedient to God's commands.
3. Trust that people will respond to the power that is in God and his message.

Bible Talk #20

Listen and Do

 Play "Name That Tune" with a CD player. Play popular songs or television jingles, etc.

Q: What is the key to doing well in this game?
- Listening!

James 1:19-25 Recap.

This is a practical book, not written to any specific church but to disciples everywhere. It talks about overcoming tough times, being blessed by God, how to be stable, fighting temptations and other vital topics that are important in living the Christian life. Let's discuss together this vital topic of listening!

Listening!
Q: What is the key to being a great listener?
- Not having presupposed ideas or prejudging (like being on a jury)
- Understanding the demeanor of the person (body language, etc.)
- Understanding the full scope of where the person is coming from (such as a spouse or child, etc.)

The same thing applies to the word of God.

Q: What keeps us from being great listeners to the word of God?
- Past experiences, already formed opinions, traditions, upbringing

The word of God can save you. (v21)
Listening to and accepting the word of God is crucial to your salvation!

Mirror analogy (v22-25)
Q: Why is the Bible compared to a mirror?
- It reveals who we are, lets us see ourselves as we really are, and exposes the inside, whether we want to see it or not. Most people do not want to be exposed. Have you ever seen anyone caught on a hidden camera. People generally hate for their thoughts and actions to be exposed.

Q: How can you tell when someone doesn't want to obey God's word?
- Very simple–they don't obey it!

Q: How do we respond when we hear the Word, but have no intention of obeying it?
- That was a "nice" sermon.
- That was a "nice" Bible talk.
- I'm not sure the scripture actually means that?
- It's a great topic, I need to learn more about how to apply it, etc.

39

Q: What are some excuses we use for not obeying?
- There are no absolutes, that was then, this is now, my family...
- I'm a special case, I didn't like the way he said it to me...
- You can't take it literally, I don't think a loving God would...

Foolish! When we do this, we are saying: "That's nice, God, but here is what I think would be a better idea..."

What are our only options?
1. Continue to be foolish
2. Break the mirror (the Bible)
3, Do something about it–Change!

Q: How can we put the Bible into practice with our spouses and children?

Q: How can we put the Bible into practice in our dating relationships?

Q: How can we put the Bible into practice in our personality and character development?

Share some examples of people who have listened to God and his word and have radically changed.

The word of God will judge us. Rejecting God's word is exactly the same as rejecting Jesus himself!

God tells us right up front what to listen for and put into practice. He has no hidden agenda.

 It is very smart to put God's word into practice! The incredible thing is that when we put God's word into practice, it not only prepares us for judgment day, but it makes our lives better in every area!

Are you listening to and obeying God's word in your daily lives?

Bible Talk #21

Are You in Touch?

 OPENER Have everyone in the group share one good quality and one bad quality about themselves.

Q: Do you think you have an accurate assessment of yourself? (In touch)

Q: Is it possible you have an inaccurate assessment of yourself? (Out of touch)
- Yes. Distorted, too optimistic, too pessimistic, etc.

Q. Has another person ever had an inaccurate assessment of you? When?
- We can have a distorted view of ourselves, and other people can certainly have a warped assessment of us as well.

Q: What is the true assessment of who you are?
- What God thinks–His view is the correct view; it is unbiased and it counts.

Q: Do you think most people have an accurate view of themselves?

This study is entitled "Are You in Touch?" We will look at two people. One was very in touch, and one was out of touch.

 Lesson Scripture **Luke 7:36-50** (Story of the Sinful Woman) Recap.

Q: What kind of reputation did the woman have?
- Public reputation as a sinner! Perhaps a prostitute, adulteress, town drunk, gossip, busybody, etc.

Q: What did she risk by coming to Jesus?
- Her pride, her self-worth, and every shred of dignity she had left

Q: How did this woman demonstrate humility?
- Just coming to the Pharisee's house, overcoming her fears and doubts
- Crying and weeping in front of all those people
- Washing Jesus' feet with her hair, kissing his feet, anointing his feet with perfume

Q: Why did she humble herself?
- She had an accurate view of who she was and of who Jesus was!
- She was in touch with where she stood in relationship to God.

This is a sharp woman. She has a clear picture of her state before God.
The Bible says all have sinned and fallen short of the glory of God. (Romans 3:23)
The Bible says the wages of sin is death–separation from God. (Romans 6:23)
Without God, we are all in big trouble. We need God desperately.
This woman clearly saw her need for Jesus.

Q: What was Simon the Pharisee's attitude?
- Critical of the woman, critical of Jesus
- Sarcastic, negative, cynical, judgmental, and above all, prideful

Q. How did Simon demonstrate pride?
- He didn't do anything for Jesus, was not focused on the needs of others
- He was totally self-focused; he had a critical, unloving attitude
- He should have been excited about the woman's repentance, but wasn't
- He was blind to what was really going on–pride blinds

Q: Were the woman's sins worse than Simon's?
- No, just more visible. But Simon thought that hers were much worse.

Q: How are we like Simon in our attitudes?
- Prideful, self-focused
- Out of touch with who we really are, with how we compare with Jesus
- Act like everything is fine, we're doing great
- Criticize others who are humble and getting their lives right with God
- Threatened by righteous or humble people

Q: How would we act if we were in touch with our sin?
- Be humble about what kind of sinners we really are
- Be merciful, loving, forgiving of other people
- Be broken-hearted about how our sin has hurt God and hurt others
- Be concerned about what God thinks, not about what other people think

Q: So how do we get in touch?
- Stop comparing yourself with people and compare yourself with Jesus
- Get some spiritual people in your life who will tell you the truth
- Read the Bible, study God's word to see how God views your character

Start making the effort to get in touch.
Be encouraged by the faith and courage of the sinful woman.

Mary–Woman of Faith

 Go around the room and ask: "Can I borrow...?"
$20.00? Your car for the week? Your house for a party?
Your wedding ring for a day? Your child for the weekend?
Your house for my family to stay in for a month? One of your kidneys?

Ask the group to imagine if a total stranger asked these same questions of them.

Q: What factors do you consider in deciding whether or not to comply?
• Need, motive, purpose for what they want, how much you trust them

The greater the request, the more difficult it is to say yes.
We weigh things out more, scrutinizing the need and the motive.

Let's look at a woman who had a stranger ask to borrow something!

 Luke 1:26-39 (Mary) Recap.

Q: What did God want to borrow from Mary?
• Her womb, her time, her energy, her life

Q: How do you think this might have disrupted her schedule and plans?

Q: How might Mary have reacted to this request?
• Big commitment, too inconvenient
• "Let me think about it, analyze it"
• "Let me offer a better plan, this one is a little embarrassing"
• "No! It's too much to ask..."
• "Alright, if I have to..." (angry or resigned to it)

Q: What was Mary's reaction? Her attitude?
• "May it be to me as you have said." **(Luke 1:38)**

Q: How do most people define faith? How do we know tht Mary responded with faith?
• She believed the angel.
• She trusted God completely.
• She obeyed.

The Bible defines faith differently from how most people define it.
Faith=belief=trust=action and obedience.

No action, **No faith.** No obedience, **No faith.**

You can break faith down into three steps:
1. Knowledge of the facts
2. Conviction that the facts have personal relevance
3. Actions based on your convictions

Example: You have a bad toothache and need a dentist. I tell you that I have experience with toothaches and can fix your bad tooth.

Step One: You believe I have experience with fixing toothaches.

Q: Does this knowledge fix your toothache? No!

Step Two: You believe that I can fix your toothache.

Q: Does this belief fix your toothache? No!

Step Three: You sit down in my chair and let me work on your tooth. Only now does the toothache get fixed–when there is action!

Notice Mary's faith: Believed the facts, believed what it meant for her life, and then obeyed! She could have stopped short.

Q: The angel asked a lot of Mary. What does God ask of us?
- Obedience, commitment, relationship with him, make Jesus Lord
- Faithfulness to God, commitment to the church, everything!
- God wants it all–This is what "Jesus is Lord" means

Q: How did you respond when you first found out what God expected of you?

Q: What kind of response does God want?
- Whatever God wants, we need to be ready to accept it and do it! **(Luke 1:38)**

Notice verse 34, Mary asked questions and wanted an explanation, but she didn't demand to know everything before she obeyed.

Q: In what ways do we need to imitate Mary?
- Live a righteous life so God will want to use us
- Ask questions, but trust God and obey
- Overcome fears, doubts, skepticism

 Have the faith of Mary. Trust and obey God.

Make Every Effort

 Game: Liar's Club. Get three hard-to-identify objects and three "liars." Prepare the liars by telling them the true function of each of the objects. Then have one of the liars correctly describe the name and function of an object, and have the other two try to fool the people in the room. After each object is described, have people vote on which "liar" is telling the truth.

Q: Those of you who were fooled, how do you feel?

Q: Have you ever been deceived before? How? How did you feel?

We all have been fooled at one time or another, and it is no fun. So tonight let's dig into God's word and see if we can prevent being fooled about a very crucial subject.

 Luke 13:22-30 and **Matthew 7:13-14** (The wide and narrow door) Recap.

Q: Why did they ask this question?
• It's a very important question!

Q: What is the narrow door/narrow way?
• The entrance to heaven, salvation, eternal life
• The entrance to the kingdom of God, the new birth, a joyful life

Q: What is the wide door/broad way?
• The entrance to sin, miserable life, destruction, hell

Q: What makes the narrow door/narrow way so narrow?
• It's hard to find.
• It's demanding. People don't want to live a life of self-denial and put Jesus first.
• It's hard work. People don't want to have to work hard. People tend to be lazy.

Q: What makes the wide door/broad way so broad?
• It's the path of default–do nothing, and you can remain on the broad way.
• It looks more attractive. Wine, women and song. Fun in the sun. Eat, drink and be merry.
• It's easier. Most people are lazy and want the easy road.

The Bible says Satan is a liar, a murderer and a deceiver.
By definition, if you are being deceived, you don't know it. If you were aware of the deception, you wouldn't be deceived.

We have talked a little about the nature of the wide and narrow ways, but...

Q: If you were Satan, how would you deceive people to keep them on the wide way and off the narrow way (be creative and have some fun)?
• Make many doors to discourage true seekers
• Put persuasive doorkeepers at each door to convince people that this is the correct and only door they should enter

- Make the narrow way seem very, very, very narrow, impossible to enter
- Appoint someone to tell people every door leads into the same house
- Put some people on the broad way to tell everyone how great it is
- Put people on the supposed narrow way who are miserable, depressed, negative, critical, downtrodden and love to talk about it
- Tell people there is no hurry, take your time, relax
- Present a third alternative: "good" narrow road for priests, "evil" narrow road for murderers, wide road in the middle for the rest of us good folks

Q: What is the problem with the "Three Road" mentality?
- The middle road and evil, narrow road lead to the same place.

Q: Is the narrow door/narrow way worth the effort?
- Of course

Read **Luke 13:24.**

Q: How hard is the narrow door/narrow way to find?

Q: What conclusions can you draw from Jesus' words?
- Make every effort!

Q: How much effort is "every" effort?
- Every, all consuming, first priority, most important
- It should be obvious to all, nothing else in your life is as important

Q: What kind of effort would you make if you lost your child or sibling?

Notice that many will even try to enter, but will not be able to!

Q: What does that tell you?
- The gate is narrower than most people think.
- Many religious people are going to be surprised.

Read **Luke 13:28.**

Q: What kind of picture does this paint?
- Anger at self, frustration, strong emotion
- "Why didn't I work harder at finding the gate?...If only I had..."

Q: How do you know if you are making every effort?
- Reading, praying, asking, learning, seeking...it should be obvious!

1. Don't be deceived about the worth of the narrow road.
2. Don't be deceived about how hard it is to find the way.
3. Make every effort to find it!

Don't Miss Out

Play a game called "Please Excuse Me." Compile a list of very appealing invitations to upcoming fictitious events:

- Would you come over this Saturday for steak and lobster?
- I have an extra ticket to Hawaii. Would you like to go with us?
- The governor wants to have dinner with us, can you also come? etc.

Go around the room and make an invitation to each person. They are to make up an outrageous, ridiculous excuse for not accepting your invite. The most absurd, funny, outlandish, ridiculous excuse wins a prize.

Q: Has any one of you ever been given a flimsy excuse? When? How did it feel?

It's one thing for someone to give a flimsy excuse for not helping clean your garage or paint your house, but it would be odd to give an excuse to get out of something like a trip to Hawaii.

Let's take a look at a parable Jesus told about a similar situation.

Luke 14:15-23 Recap.

Q: What was this banquet going to be like?
- This was going to be an incredible banquet.

A parable illustrates a great spiritual truth.

Q: The man giving the banquet is obviously God, but what does the banquet represent?
- The kingdom of God, which is available now.
- We can be a part of the kingdom of God now. We don't have to wait till we die.

Q: What makes the banquet (kingdom) great? What is on the menu?
- Friendships, great marriages, obedient children, forgiveness of sins, freedom from guilt, relationship with God, peace, joy, purpose, etc.

Q: What comes to mind when you think of American "Christianity"?
- Dull, boring, ritualistic, oppressive, hypocritical, tradition-bound, etc.

It is obvious tthat Jesus' description of the great banquet and what is happening in "American Christianity" don't match up.

Q: What conclusion may be drawn?
- What we see in "American Christianity" is not the great banquet.

Q: Why do people miss out on the great banquet that God offers?
- Skeptical, cynical, fearful
- Haven't been invited
- Don't want to disrupt their schedule, it isn't convenient
- Have gone to what they thought was the banquet and were disappointed

e.g. If I offered you steak and fed you shoe leather, the next time someone invited you for steak, you wouldn't be very excited about it.

Q: What can you tell about the master from this parable?
- Generous, loving, planned out great things for those who accepted the invitation
- Doesn't want anyone to miss out

Note that there were some conditions on the invitation: had to show up on the right day, at the right time, at the right place, etc; but this was nothing compared to what was being offered.

Q: Who are the blind, poor, lame, etc.? We are!

Q: What is the right response to being invited to something exclusive?
- Humility! "Wow! I'm honored. Yes, I would love to come. What do I bring?"

This is the response we need to have to the invitation of Jesus!

Q: What did you think of the excuses we made in the excuse game?

Q: What do you think of the excuses made by the people in this parable?

Q: What excuses do we give to Jesus' invitation?
- Busy, not convenient, too much going on right now
- I don't know enough about what is being offered
- I'm not sure how good the banquet is going to be
- I'm tired

Some of you are making pretty flimsy excuses to not respond to God.

 God doesn't want you to miss any of the blessings that he has in store for you. God's kingdom is filled with incredible gifts. Ask the person who brought you about what they are feasting on in the kingdom of God.

Stop making flimsy excuses for missing this festive banquet.
Don't miss out!

Real Followers Only

Show a video clip or two of something entertaining.

Q: What is your favorite form of entertainment?

Q: Who is your favorite entertainer?

Q: What makes something/someone entertaining?

Q: What is the one big drawback of entertainment? It doesn't last!

Read **John 6:16-69.** Recap.

Background: Jesus had been doing many miracles and had gathered a rather large following.

Q: If you only read verses 16-24, what would you say about this crowd?
- They are committed and saved.

Yet, look at their real hearts! (Jesus did!)

Q: What are some of the reasons that people were following Jesus?
- To watch the miracles
- See Jesus do verbal battle with his opponents
- Get food
- Get healed
- Hear him preach/be entertained by the spectacle of it all
- Enjoy the fellowship of the large crowds

Q: What are some of the same reasons people follow Christianity?
- Tradition, friends, social activities, choirs, buildings, etc.

Jesus challenged the peoples' commitment (v26).

The definition of a real follower is seen in vv35 and 53.

Q: What does verse 53 mean?
- Engulf Jesus
- Be consumed with Jesus
- Describes someone who makes Jesus their very life

e.g.. "He eats, drinks and sleeps football," means "he is totally consumed with the game of football."

Real disciples have more than a passing interest in Jesus, they are consumed!

Q: How did the crowds react to the challenge of Jesus?
- They got defensive. (v28)
- They didn't understand it. (vv41-44)
- They argued sharply about it. (v52)
- They turned their backs and stopped following him. (v66)

Q: How do these reactions reveal the condition of their hearts?

Q: What is significant in verse 67?
- Jesus gave even the twelve an opportunity to leave.

Q: What does this tell you about who Jesus wants as followers?
- Wholehearted volunteers only–No force or coercion or because they "have to."

Q: What is the right reaction to the challenges of Jesus?
- Peter chooses to stay with Jesus. (vv67-69)

 Why are you a "Christian"? Why are you here (at the Bible talk)? Peter's heart should be our heart! I may not totally understand everything, but I trust God.

If your heart is not right, or if it has drifted from this, don't quit.
Just get it right and remember Jesus wants only real followers!

Bible Talk #26

The Value of the Kingdom

Q: What is something valuable that you own?

Q: What makes it valuable to you?

Q: What qualities make something valuable?
- Costly, rare, irreplaceable, sentimental value, precious to you, one of a kind, beauty, etc.

Q: Do you have an eye for value? What are you good at evaluating?

Let's look at a story that Jesus told about some items of value.

Matthew 13:44-46 Recap.

Q: Is the kingdom of heaven available now, or do we have to wait for heaven?
- The kingdom of heaven is where Jesus is king. It is the family of God! (If necessary, read **Colossians 1:13-14.** We have been brought into the kingdom.)

In fact, the kingdom and the church are one and the same. Heaven will be great, but God's blessings can be enjoyed now.

Q: Describe the pearl in vv45-46. How big? How shiny? How beautiful?

Q: Did the man know anything about pearls?
- Yes! He was a pearl merchant.

Q: Did the pearl merchant get a good deal?

Q: Describe the treasure in the field in v44?

Q: Was the man out looking for treasure?
- No, he stumbled onto it.

Q: Did the man get a good deal?
- Yes! In his joy, he sold all he had to obtain it.

Q: How do you act when you aren't sure if you are getting a good business deal?
- Tentative, wondering, hesitant

Q: Were these men hesitant or tentative?
- No way!

Q: Were these men willing to sell everything they had?
- They were totally confident that they were getting a great deal.
- It wasn't even debatable.
- If you had a balance scale and put the treasure or the pearl on one side and all their possessions on the other, the scale wouldn't gently tip. It would crash down.

Jesus is making the point about how valuable the kingdom of God is.

Q: How was Jesus so sure?

Q: What are the benefits of the kingdom that make it so valuable?
- Relationship with God, spouse that loves God first, obedient children, friends, peace, forgiveness of sins, freedom from guilt, etc.

Q: How do you know if someone values something?
- Protect it, care for it, wash it, pamper it, show it off, talk about it

Q: How do most people value the kingdom of God?
- Negative, cynical, think of it as powerless, contemptible, etc.

Q: How do most "Christians" look at their churches?
- Flippant, criticize them, go when they can, casual, no big deal
- Hop from church to church, hard to please, treat with contempt

Q: Why do so few people see the value of the kingdom (the church)?
- Never seen it
- Have seen "false pearls" and been disappointed

e.g. If you were promised a "great ballet" and saw a jr. high production of *The Nutcracker,* you would never again accept an invitation to see a ballet.

Q: Describe a church that is the way the Bible describes it?
- Loving, growing, meeting needs, forgiving, exciting, powerful, etc.

Q: What would such a church be worth?

Is the kingdom valuable to you? Do you see its real worth? Would you give up everything you own for the kingdom? If you are skeptical, doubting, unsure, then the problem is that you don't clearly see the value of God's kingdom.

Bible Talk #27   The Church

 Q: As a child, what was your favorite thing about church?

Q: As a child, what was your least favorite thing about church?

Q: In today's world, what do most people think the church is?
* A building, etc.

Q: What turns most people off about church today?
* Social club, clothes, money, prestige
* Hypocrites
* Traditions
* Always talk about money
* Sports–which church has the best softball or volleyball team, etc.
* Just a place to meet nice girls
* Prejudicial
* Boring
* Sermons not practical–changes with society, don't even open a Bible

 Lesson Scripture Read **Acts 2:42-47**. Recap.

Here the Bible describes what the true church should be like, and it is anything but boring!

This scripture gives a blueprint of what the church today should be like. Let's look at how exciting church can be.

Acts 2:42 says they devoted themselves ("devoted" means "addicted," "committed"). Discuss each characteristic and contrast it to the world's opinion of church.

1. To the apostles' teaching–They were committed to the Bible.

2. To the fellowship–They were committed to each other.

3. To the breaking of bread–They were committed to remembering Jesus.

4. To prayer–They were committed to constant communication with God.

5. Meeting the needs of everyone–They were committed to helping each other.

6. Were together and had everything in common–They were committed to unity.

7. Met together regularly–They were committed to being together!

8. People were being added to their number daily–They were committed to everyone getting a chance to be a part of this great church.

 Conclusion Does this sound like the church you grew up in, or even the one you attend now? This is the blueprint for the kind of church you should seek to be in. This is the kind of church God wants.

Career Night

OPENER Q: **If you could do it over again, what career would you most like to go into?**

In the Christian life, you have the exciting privilege of living out qualities of character that are emulated in several professions. Let's look at them together and compare our characters to them.

Lesson Scripture Read **2 Timothy 1:8-2:15.** Recap.

1. **A Prisoner** (v1:8) Discuss the qualities of a prisoner.
   - Totally dependent on others, at the mercy of others, must be willing to suffer at the hands of others, not in control of his time or agenda

2. **A Teacher** (v2:1) Discuss the qualities of a teacher.
   - Reliable, qualified, speaks the truth, corrects misconceptions, longsuffering, patient, looks out for the interest of the student.

3. **The Soldier** (v2:3) Discuss the qualities of a soldier.
   - Follows orders, unquestioning loyalty, fight for what is right, willing to be involved in life and death situations, well-trained, disciplined, bold

4. **The Athlete** (v2:5) Discuss the qualities of an athlete.
   - Regimented, daily training, goals, trains for progress, runs according to the rules, runs to win the prize, self-motivated but also willing to be coached and trained

5. **The Farmer** (v2:6) Discuss the qualities of a farmer.
   - Patient, willing to work long hours, has hope, can't see the immediate results, cares for the crops, deals with the weeds

6. **The Workman** (v2:14) Discuss the qualities of a workman.
   - Dependable, at times overlooked or taken for granted, willing to do the dirty work, satisfied with a job well done

Conclusion All of these qualities of character are available to us in the Christian life. Even if we missed out on them early in life, we have the chance to put these qualities into our characters.

Naaman

Lesson Scripture   **2 Kings 5:1-16** Recap.

Q: Who was Naaman?
- Commander of the army of the King of Aram and a great soldier

Naaman was a great soldier but he also had leprosy. Describe leprosy for those not familiar with it.

1. Read **2 Kings 5:2-6.** (Naaman goes to the king.)
Q: Why does Naaman take so much treasure to the king of Israel?
- Leprosy was a terrible disease and he would pay any cost to be rid of it.
Q: What was the king of Israel's response?
- "Am I God? Can I kill and bring back to life?"
Q: What would you send to be healed?

2. Read **2 Kings 5:8-10.** (Elisha's response)
Q: What does Elisha tell him?
- Send him to me so he will know that there is a prophet in Israel.
Q: Why do you think Elisha sent a messenger out to Naaman?
- Perhaps to show the power of God is in obedience and not in a man.
Q: Where do we find God's cure today to be healed?
- In the word of God

3. Read **2 Kings 5:11-12.** (Naaman's response to Elisha)
Q: Why did Naaman not initially obey Elisha's request?
- He wanted some public spectacle of healing.
- He wanted to be healed in the way he thought was best.
Q: What keeps us from obeying God's word today?
- We think we know a better way.
Q: Have you ever gone off mad at God over what he expects of you?

4. Read **2 Kings 5:13-16.** (Naaman's obedience)
Q: What kind of attitude did Naaman now have?
- Submissive, humble, repentant, obedient
Q: What should our attitude be toward God's word today?
- Submissive, humble, repentant, obedient
Q: What cured Naaman?
- Simple trusting, obedience!
Q: How did Naaman respond to being healed?
- He committed himself to serving no one but the God of Israel.

Conclusion   Like Naaman we can have preconceived ideas about what God should do. We need to shed those ideas and trust and obey God. Our relationship with God begins with faith and obedience.

Bible Talk #30

One Burning Question

 OPENER Imagine that Jesus himself has dropped in for a ten-minute visit to your group. You may ask him any question you want, but only one!

Q: What question would you ask?

Q: Why that particular question?

On one occasion, a man had the chance to ask that "one burning question."

 Lesson Scripture **Mark 10:17-31** Recap.

Q: What can we tell about this man?
- Rich, religious, respectful, righteous, eager

In Luke 18, the Bible records that he was a leader.

Q: What does it take to be a leader?
- Smart, sharp, organized, persuasive, confident, friendly

Q: If you met this man in the mall, what would he be like?
- Friendly, sharp, nice car, intelligent, church-going, great guy

Today we might describe this man as someone who: Prays and reads his Bible, goes to church, active in the community, doesn't drink or smoke or sleep around, a business leader, etc.

Q: Wouldn't you assume that someone like this would be going to heaven?

Read verse 24.

Q: What were the disciples' reactions? Why?
- If this man can't make it, then who can?

Q: What did you notice about the questions we all wanted to ask Jesus?

Q: What do you notice about the question of the rich young ruler?
- Direct and dangerous
- Do we have the courage to want to really know the answer?

Notice verse 21. Jesus looked at him and loved him. Jesus wasn't being mean or harsh. Jesus looked at him and said, "One thing you lack." (Good friends tell you the truth.)

Q: What kept this young man out of heaven? Was it strictly love of money?
- He wasn't sold out to God. He wasn't willing to give God everything.
- His money was the one thing that stood between him and God.

Q: Why was it so important that the man be totally sold out to God?
- Jesus wants all of your heart, not part of it–not even most of it.
- If he isn't Lord of all, he isn't Lord at all.
- There is no such thing as a part-time disciple or ninety percent commitment.

Q: How would you like it if your spouse was ninety percent committed to you, or unfaithful only once a year?

The rich young ruler thought he was doing great, but he wasn't. He was fooled.

Q: How do we get faked into thinking we are doing great spiritually?
- Compare ourselves to others instead of to Jesus
- Obey people/leaders instead of God's word
- Do all the religious, ritualistic things, and think we're fine

For the rich young ruler, it was his wealth that stood between him and God.

Q: What things do we let stand between us and a relationship with God?
- Business, job, hobbies, free time, security, independence, relationships, etc.

Q: What did the rich young ruler forfeit?
- Heaven, rich life, a life of purpose and mission

The rich young ruler made a very poor choice. He kept his money, but lost his life.

Read verses 29-31.
You never lose out when you give something up for God. You can never outgive God.

If Jesus looked at you and said, "One thing you lack," what would he say is that "one thing" that stands between you and God? Would it be your time, prestige, selfishness, career, hobbies, sports or your sin?

In comparison to what God is ready to give us, are these things worth hanging on to?

 It takes more than just being religious to be right with God. Don't let anyone stand in the way of your commitment to Jesus. Don't let "one thing" hold you back from a relationship with God.

Bible Talk #31

Seek Real Treasure

 OPENER Q: **What is the American dream?**
- New home, car, computer, hefty bank account, etc.

Jesus was incredible. He knew two thousand years ago that people today would still wrestle with riches and materialism.

 Lesson Scripture **Matthew 6:19-24** Recap.

Q: **What types of things do we consider riches?**

Q: **What sorts of things do moths and rust destroy?**

Q: **What can thieves break in and steal?**

Jesus was very direct. This was not a suggestion, but a command:
Do not store up treasure on earth. Jesus was the ultimate authority on what lasts forever–and earthly treasures do not last.
Let's look at three things that treasures on earth will do.

1. Treasure disintegrates.
Q: **Have you ever bought anything that disintegrated? Broke? Wore out?**

As nice as it may start out to be, things break, wear, tear, scratch, etc.

Q: **What happens if your self-worth is wrapped up in this thing?**

2. Treasure disappoints.
Q: **Have you ever bought anything from a television infomercial?**

Q: **How did it work? Did you get what you expected?**

Q: **Have you ever bought something you thought would make you cool, attractive? Did it?**

e.g. I thought when I got a motorcycle, I would be able to get lots of dates. We've all bought things that ended up disappointing us because they do not deliver the fulfillment they promise.

It's bad that treasure disintegrates and bad that it disappoints, but the worst thing about treasures are that they distract us.

3. Treasure distracts.
Q: **Have you ever invested in something?**

Q: **How much time did you invest in keeping up with it?**

Q: **Did you ever buy a new car or motorcycle? How much effort did it take?**

Q: What did Jesus mean by "where your treasure is, there your heart will be"?
- Your heart follows your investment.
- You will give time and attention to the things most important to you.

Q: Where do we invest ourselves?
- Stocks, bonds, cars, houses, hobbies, sports, jobs, relationships, education

Q: Are these things all bad?
- No–But they do have the potential to lead us away from God.

Q: Have you ever been distracted from God by an earthly treasure?

God wants your heart. He is hurt when you don't pay attention to him.
e.g. I'm hurt when my kids would rather spend time on games or toys instead of with me.

Reread verse 20.

Q: What does Jesus mean "store up in heaven"?
- Invest yourself in things that will last and are eternal
- Things that won't disintegrate, disappoint, distract

Q: What are some treasures that we can store up in heaven?
- Bringing others to God, serving others in need, doing good deeds, etc.

Q: How can you tell what is important to someone?
- Look at how much time and effort they give to it.

Q: What does Jesus mean when he says "no one can serve two masters"?
- Choose one or the other, can't do both
- Must make a conscious decision

Q: How can you tell which decision someone has made?
- Watch their life, look at a person's checkbook and daytimer, it will show

Who have you helped become a Christian? What treasures have you sent ahead?

Q: How can you tell when someone is devoted to God?
- Read their Bible, pray, talk about God, share what God is doing in their lives, serve others, etc.
- Want to be with God and God's people

 Are you devoted to things, or the one who made the things?
Are you storing up treasure in a safe place, or will yours get eaten by moths, destroyed by rust and stolen by thieves?
Are the most important things in your life things that disintegrate, disappoint, and distract you from God?
Start storing up treasures in heaven, where they will be waiting for you!

Fruit Inspectors

 OPENER Q: If you were a fruit, what would you be and why?
  • We use the analogy of fruit in our speech often.

Q: What expressions can you think of that use fruit in them?
  • Sour grapes, apple of my eye, "she's a peach," it was a fruitful meeting, the car was in cherry condition, effort I put in bore fruit, etc.

The Bible talks a lot about fruit: the fruit of the spirit, being fruitful, bearing fruit in every good work. On a number of occasions, Jesus used fruit to illustrate a spiritual principle.

 Lesson Scripture Read **Matthew 7:15-23.** Recap.

Q: If you came upon a tree bearing a sign that said, "sweet, juicy apple tree," how would you know if the sign was true?
  • You would try the tree's fruit.

Q: Does the sign make any difference in the taste of the fruit?
  • No, the fruit is what it is.

Q: How do we hang signs on ourselves?
  • Claim "I'm a Christian," claim Jesus is Lord, claim to be a follower of Jesus

Q: How do you know if someone's claim is true?
  • Watch their fruit (v16)–Everyone bears fruit, whether good or bad.

Q: What makes the fruit good or bad?
  • Jesus said it's the tree, the source of the fruit (v17).

Q: What is the source of our actions or our fruits?
  • Our hearts, where all the actions begin

Reread verse 15.

Q: What comes to mind when you think of a false prophet?
  • Demonic, sinister-looking person, evil, mean, cold, deceitful

Q: How did Jesus say that they would appear?
  • Like sheep–They look good, gentle, loving etc.

Q: How can you tell a false prophet? Reread verses 16-20.
  • Everyone bears fruit in their lives–in their actions, either good or bad.

Q: What are some good fruits?
  • Love, joy, kindness, self-control, humility, patience, obedient children, great marriages, sharing Jesus with a friend, great friendships, great relationships, being selfless, serving, giving, loving, etc.

Q: What are some bad fruits?
- Selfishness, adultery, pride, anger, impurity, jealousy, rebellion, lust, deceit, hypocrisy, greed, hatred, immorality, fits of rage, idolatry, etc.

The fruits are gross. They stink and are repulsive, putrid and rotten!

Q: Where do these fruits originate?
- The heart–We act from the overflow of the heart.

Reread verses 21-23.

Q: What kind of people were these? Religious

Q: How do you know? They said, "Lord, Lord."

Q: What kinds of fruits had they born? Miracles, cast out demons, etc.

Q: What was the problem?
- They had bad hearts. They had a few good deeds, but they were rebellious. They were disobedient to God; they didn't know God (v21). They seemed to be such religious people, but God called them "evildoers."

Q: Why was Jesus so hard on them?
- They weren't obedient. He wants us to trust and obey.

So many religious people do just what they want. They rationalize, minimize and explain away even the simplest commands in the Bible. e.g. Go make disciples, deny yourselves, take up your cross, repent and be baptized, etc.

These people looked good, but their fruit was rotten. It stunk of rebellion!

Q: How do we look good, yet rebel against God?
- Go to church, yet hate it
- Read our Bibles, but don't obey it
- Act religious, but have hearts and lives full of sin, etc.

Q: What can we do to make sure we don't end up like this rebellious group?
- Get into the word, find out what God expects and obey it
- Change our hearts and obey God, no matter what he asks

Q: Do you think these religious people were suprised?
- You bet! They thought they were fine, but they were lost.

Conclusion
1. Don't be caught unaware. Don't be surprised!
2. Let someone inspect your fruit.
3. If you have rebellion, let someone help you deal with it.

Bible Talk #33

Practice What You Preach

 Psychiatrists sometimes use inkblots to see what kinds of associations people make out of random blots of ink. Let's play a verbal inkblot game.

Q: What is the first thought or image that comes to mind when I say:
- Taxes, senators, Mercedes, fast food, Las Vegas, computers, old age, church and religion. (Take a lot of responses from the last two.)

Q: Would you say that most peoples' initial thoughts about religion are good?
Q: Based on your experience with religion, how would you characterize it in general terms?
- American "Christianity" is in a sad state of affairs. Many leaders are corrupt, greedy, weak, etc. The Bible is used to promote pet doctrines, or only used occasionally. Churches are "lukewarm" and not much different from the rest of the world. Churches are dying, ritualistic, tradition-bound and swayed by the norms of society. God is left out and made to look weak or indifferent, a cream puff or a tyrant. "Christians" are disillusioned, cynical, apathetic, uncommitted, materialistic or lukewarm.

When Jesus came on the scene two thousand years ago, things were not much different. On one occasion, Jesus gave a "State of Religion" address.

 Matthew 23:1-39 Recap.

This passage is recorded in the Bible for a reason, so we can learn from it. We learn how to be true disciples, and not just religious people.

They do not practice what they preach (v3).

Q: What is this called?
- Hypocrite

Q: How did these religious people get caught up in hypocrisy?
- Let tradition and ritual replace God's teaching
- Greed or materialism overshadow their commitment
- Compromised with sin so they wouldn't look narrow-minded
- More interested in how they looked than in being righteous

Q: Why was Jesus so upset with their hypocrisy?
- Sounded like the truth, but it was a lie
- Had religion draped all over it, but it wasn't loving
- Done in God's name, but it wasn't what God wanted
- Lacked sincerity, their hearts were not in it

Q: How do we get caught up in hypocrisy?
- Don't know the Bible, don't read it, and don't put it into practice
- Let tradition and ritual replace God's plan for our lives
- We become lazy and lukewarm
- We are more interested in how we look than in being righteous

There are two ways to avoid hypocrisy, one is wimpy and the other is hard work.

Q: What are two ways that we can avoid being a hypocrite?
- Totally run from God, the truth, the Bible, commitment and righteousness
- Decide to obey God and do what God wants, no matter the consequences

Q: What makes the latter decision so hard?
- Must study to find out what God wants (not necessarily what people say)
- Most religious people won't like it
- You catch grief every time you make a mistake
- Its much harder to be righteous than to appear righteous

To avoid being a hypocrite takes incredible humility!

Q: Why would that be true?
- React with humility when a flaw or problem is pointed out, don't be defensive. (How did the Pharisees react when Jesus pointed out their flaws?)
- Be open about your shortcomings and the areas you are still working on.
- They compromised with sin so they wouldn't look narrow-minded.
- Be teachable, ready to change anything God wants you to change.
- We need people intimately involved in our lives to help us see our weaknesses.
- We must be open to what the Bible teaches, even if it is different than what we were previously taught or from our backgrounds.

If the Pharisees had been humble, they would have accepted Jesus' words and changed. They would no longer have been hypocrites.

Don't be a wimp and run away from the truth.
Decide to be a truth seeker, no matter what the consequences.
Be humble and get someone in your life to tell you the truth about what they see.

Be diligent. Follow the Bible above human teachers and traditions.

Bible Talk #34

Jesus Heals the Paralytic

OPENER Q: What handicap would be the most difficult for you to handle? Why?

It's easy to think of handicapped people as helpless, but we are going to look at a handicapped man who was far from helpless.

Lesson Scripture Luke 5:17-26 Recap.

Imagine a packed house for this Bible Talk. The room is full of religious leaders like Billy Graham, Reverend Jesse Jackson, the Pope...

Q: How would you feel about leading the Bible talk?
- Intimidated, scared, nervous...

Q: What would you pick as the topic? Why?
- Something nice, general, not too controversial

As you are teaching, the plaster starts falling from the ceiling. Men up on the roof are ripping the ceiling apart. Down through the ceiling, a paralyzed man is lowered on a mat.

Q: What would be going through your mind right now?

Q: What do you know about this paralyzed man?
- He had some truly loyal friends.
- They were determined, assertive and persistent.
- Along with his friends, he had incredible faith.

Read verse 20. "Friend, your sins are forgiven."

Q: If you were one of Jesus' disciples, what would you be thinking right now?
- "Oh no, Jesus, don't say that. That's going to be too controversial!"
- "Jesus, that's going to start an argument, for sure."

Jesus is amazing. He is not afraid of controversy. He tells the truth.

Verse 20 says that Jesus saw their faith.

Q: What did he see?
- They were doing something about what they believed!
- It was a belief that spurred them to action.

Q: What did they believe?
- That Jesus could heal him
- It was more than intellectual belief, more than academic belief!
- Faith isn't wimpy, intellectual, armchair activity. Faith is action!

Q: What obstacles did the paralyzed man overcome to get to Jesus?
- Distance to the house, getting friends to carry him, the crowd, getting on the roof, overcoming his own doubts and fears

Q: What excuses could he have made not to get to Jesus?
- It's too far, and there are too many people.
- I've heard that he is demon-possessed.
- The Pharisees say that he is dangerous.
- He probably doesn't have time for me.

The paralyzed man overcame many obstacles to get to Jesus and to be healed.

Q: What obstacles and distractions do we need to overcome to get to Jesus?
- Fight the crowds
- Business, laziness, inconvenience, peer pressure, tradition, family bias
- Kids, work, bad experiences, previous failures, skepticism, doubt

If we need excuses to stay away from God, we can find one easily!

Q: What did Jesus think about this man's faith?
- He was impressed (v20). He called him "friend." He granted him forgiveness, and the man didn't even ask for it (vv21-22). Jesus healed the man as well.

The man went away with more than he had asked for! When we sacrifice, or make an effort toward Jesus, he always gives us more than we asked for.

Just like the man who was physically paralyzed, some of us are spiritually paralyzed.

We don't have any way to get where we want to go!
...no power over sin
...no convictions about what is right and wrong
...no way to get to heaven

Q: How do we go about getting spiritually healed?
- Reading your Bible, prayer, spending time with spiritual people
- Spending time in church, where you can be challenged to grow
- Find out what God says it takes to be healed and obey it!

Have the faith and courage of the paralyzed man.
Don't let any and every weak excuse keep you from Jesus.

Bible Talk #35

Satan Wants to Stop You

OPENER **Q: What are some of the New Year resolutions that you have made?**
- Diet, good grades, more discipline, etc.

One of the most crucial times for a resolution or a project is the very beginning.

Q: Why is that?
- The beginning is the hardest time because a routine or pattern needs to be set, obstacles need to be removed, discouragements avoided, and you must set a good foundation.

Satan realizes that also. Whether you are just starting to study about God or have been a disciple for years–Satan wants to stop you from growing.

Let's take a look at how Satan uses his best tricks to try to stop someone from beginning a very big project (saving the world!).

This will allow us to be more aware of Satan and the deceitful schemes he uses.

Lesson Scripture **Matthew 4:1-11** Read and recap.

This was the beginning of Jesus' ministry.
If he could stop Jesus, Satan wouldn't have to worry about his disciples, his miracles, his parables, or especially his death, burial and resurrection.

Trick #1–Immediate gratification

Satan asked Jesus to turn stones into bread (v3).
Note that he didn't tempt Jesus with a buffet, but with just plain bread.

Q: How does Satan trick us like this?
- Lying to solve a short-term problem
- Impure thoughts and gratification
- Laziness, instead of spending time with God
- Compromising to get along with others

Trick #2–Doubt

Satan said to Jesus, "If you are the son of God..." (vv5-6)

Q: How does doubt paralyze us?
- Sit and analyze instead of acting (paralysis of analysis)
- Lack confidence (Can I really do it?)
- "I've failed before, I'll fail again"

Trick #3–Fear of losing fame, fortune, glory

Satan tempted Jesus with power and position.

Q: How does Satan trick us this way?
- Lose your freedom
- If you don't look out for yourself, who will?
- Look at all the rules

 Satan used his best tricks on Jesus and failed. Now how about you?
Satan was so afraid of Jesus that he personally confronted him face to face.
Is Satan afraid of you and what your life could potentially accomplish?
Stop Satan before he stops you.

Practical things to do:
- Ask for help!
- Stick with the word of God
- Be kingdom focused

Bible Talk #36

Josiah Finds the Law

 OPENER Q: **Have you ever had a word that you mispronounced for years?**
   • Bison, foyer, suite, etc.

Q: **Have you ever used the wrong definition or misused a word?**
• Irregardless (no such word,) surrogate, pretentious, etc.

Q: **How do you feel when you've been using a word wrong for a long time?**

Q: **How do you handle it when you find you've been wrong?**

It is a natural response to want to be defensive or to justify your position.
It takes a strong man/woman of integrity to quickly admit wrong and embrace the truth.

Let's look at a remarkable story of a man of such integrity.

Lesson Scripture **2 Chronicles 34:1-33** (Josiah finds the Law) Recap.

   Under King David, Israel did great spiritually (1200 BC), but over the years the rulers after David began to lose their commitment to Jehovah. They eventually began to serve idols and get involved in pagan worship activities. Josiah lived around 600 BC.

Q: **How could Josiah have reacted after finding the law?**
• Ignored it, hidden it, criticized it, dimissed it based on the status quo

Q: **What pressures would have been on Josiah to ignore what he had found?**
• Different than the accepted norm
• Different than their heritage, what previous rulers had accepted
• To change was to admit he was wrong
• Financially, it was probably expensive to redo everything
• He was just a young man, didn't have the perspective, wisdom

Look at the attitude of Josiah's heart in verse 19–he tore his robes!

Q: **What does this show about Josiah's heart?**
• He wanted to please God, it hurt him that God's word had not been kept

Q: **How did God bless Josiah's decision to obey God's law?**
• God spared him from harm and disaster, God took care of him. (vv26-28)

Q: **How can we find ourselves in a situation similar to Josiah in which we "just find the law"?**
• Never read the Bible before

- Read it before, but did not understand its message
- Scripture is explained or pricks your heart, and you are now ready to obey it

Q: Have you had a scripture jump out at you like you've never seen it before?
- e.g. "Go make disciples"–I need to evangelize the world
- "Seek first the kingdom"–the church comes before my own desires
- "He who hates correction is stupid"–need to love correction from people

Q: What options do we have when we are confronted with God's truth?
- Same as Josiah had: ignore it, dismiss it, criticize it, etc.
- Obey it!

Q: What is the righteous thing to do?
- Obey God

Doing what is right always has drawbacks and consequences, and benefits.

Q: What are some of the drawbacks of doing what is right?
- Swallow your pride and admit you've been wrong
- Can incur the wrath of those who don't want things to change
- Might have to face angry family or friends who were comfortable with the way things were done in the past

Q: What are some of the benefits of doing what is right?
- Clear conscience
- Great relationship with God (Hard to have a great relationship with God if you are being disobedient)
- God will take care of you and bless you (vv26-28–God blessed Josiah)

All of us are going to be confronted with the truths in God's word for the rest of our lives.
God will reveal things to us that we have never seen.
God will challenge and help us grow in our faith.
God will refine us and mature us through his word.

- Be a man/woman of integrity.
- When you are confronted with God's truth like Josiah, imitate his conviction.
- Enjoy the benefits that come from obedience to God's word.

The Good Samaritan

OPENER Q: **Do you recall a time when you went out of your way to do a good deed?**

Q: **Who are some famous people with reputations for doing good deeds?**
- Mother Theresa, Jerry Lewis, Albert Schwietzer, Dale Carnegie, etc.

Let's look at a story about a remarkable do-gooder!

Luke 10:25-37 (The Good Samaritan) Recap.

Let's look at the three different characters mentioned in this story.

1) The robbers

Q: **What kind of people were they?**
- Vicious, mean, did deliberate harm, ruthless, violent

Q: **How do you feel about this type of person?**

Q: **What percentage of people fall into this category?**
- Small, but seems more common these days

2) The priest and the Levite

Q: **What kind of people were they?**
- Religious

Q: **What kind of reputation did they have before this incident?**
- Nice, kind, helpful (if you were the right race or color), giving, etc.

Q: **What percentage of people are like this?**
- The majority

Q: **What is the problem that Jesus is pointing out in this parable?**
- These religious leaders were indifferent. They didn't want to get involved

The Priest and the Levite were not like the robbers. They actively did no harm to their fellow man. But they didn't do anything to help their fellow man, either. They didn't love people; they loved only themselves. Their comfort and convenience were more important than the wounds of this man.

3. Good Samaritan

Q: **What kind of person was he?**
- Deeply concerned about a man who had been robbed and hurt

Q: What did he do for the hurt man?
- Helped him, got medical aid and guaranteed his bills would be met

Q: What is the big difference between the Priest/Levite and the Samaritan?
- Humility! Pride is being self-focused, self-centered, selfish, self-aware, etc. Humility is being others focused, outward focused, meeting the needs of others, etc.

Q: How did the Samaritan demonstrate humility?
- He overlooked the difference in race and religion.
- He sacrificed his own time, schedule and money.
- He went out of his way to heal and help the man.

Q: Which of the three (robber, priest/Levite, Samaritan) is the average "Christian" most like? Why?

Q: What impact do religious leaders have on our society?
- Many religious groups do harm because they neglect teaching the true message of Jesus Christ. People are harmed by being lulled into a false sense of security in their relationship with God.

Q: Do you think the priest/Levite had ever done any good deeds?
- Of course he had done some good deeds. Everyone can point to some good deeds. The question is, are you making any difference in the lives of people now?

Are you the kind of person that:
...goes to church, but never has helped anyone become a Christian?
...is known as the "nice" person on the block, but doesn't impact anyone?
...is religious, but doesn't risk, doesn't sacrifice, doesn't make a difference?

Are you more like the priest/Levite, or like the Good Samaritan? What impact are you having on people? (Who will be in heaven because of you?) Be like the Samaritan–love and make a difference!

Bible Talk #38

Go Make Disciples

 OPENER Situation: Imagine that you have been hurt badly in a car accident. You have only one minute to live. In that one minute, you write your last letter. Have everyone in the room share what they would say in their last minute of life.

Q: What did you notice about what most people said?
- Very specific and selective
  e.g. Suzy, I'll always remember you...

Q: If you were handed a letter that contained someone's last words, how would you treat the words in that letter?
- Very special, pay close attention
- Last words are significant, people usually choose them carefully

 Lesson Scripture **Matthew 28:18-20** (The final words of Jesus) Recap.

Q: What makes Jesus' last words different than most?
- He gave a command–Go make disciples.
- He was focused on the needs of others.
- He was concerned about helping people get in a relationship with God.
- Most important–Jesus told his disciples to go make disciples!

Q: If you were sent out to make disciples, how would you do it?
- (Most people would say...teach them about God, Jesus, the Bible, etc.)

Q: After you had taught them about all this, are they disciples yet?

Q: When do they become disciples?

Q: What if they believe everything you have taught them, but they don't want to put it into practice? Are they disciples?
- No–A disciple is someone who makes a commitment to follow Jesus. It's more than intellectual understanding, it's commitment!

Q: What is a disciple?
- A learner, a student, a follower, an apprentice to a master
- In carpentry: Apprentice to a Master craftsman
- In music: Student to a Master musician
- In sports: Athlete to a Coach
- In business: Trainee to a Mentor

It is someone who wants to learn, not someone who has to learn.
It involves the heart.
It is someone who wants to be just like Jesus, and obey everything Jesus commands.

Q: Who makes disciples? Just preachers, ministers or deacons?
- Disciples make disciples. This is in stark contrast to most churches.

The passage is commonly referred to as the Great Commission.

Q: What is a commission?
- A directive, a task, not "The Great Suggestion," it's a command

This was God's plan to get the message out! Disciples are excited about making disciples, they have something exciting to share. It is a privilege to share God's good news with people.

Q: Who do you baptize?
- Disciples–Not perfect people, not just anyone
- People who have made the commitment to be disciples only

This is very different from the religious world!

Q: What happens if you baptize someone who is not a disciple?
- They get wet, they feel better about themselves, but they're not saved

Q: What do you do after you baptize them?
- Teach them to obey everything!

Q: What's the difference between "teaching" someone and "teaching them to obey"?
- Preaching vs. Training
- Involves personal attention, accountability, repetition, intimacy, love, involvment, humility, etc.

Religious people get defensive, a disciple wants to be more like Jesus.
We all need to make decisions to be disciples.
We all need to be disciples and must learn to obey.
We all need to be trained and corrected as needed.
We all need to appreciate the people in our lives that God is using to train us.
We all need to answer the call to make disciples of all nations.

- Decide today to be a great disciple of Jesus.
- Decide today to obey the Great Commission, and go make disciples.
- Decide to be thankful for the people that God has put in our lives to help us grow and mature.

Bible Talk #39

Parable of the Soils

 OPENER Fewer and fewer people in our society today have lived on farms. Have people share what it must be like to live on a farm.

 Lesson Scripture **Matthew 13:1-9, 18-23** Recap.
A parable is a way of conveying a spiritual message from a practical episode of life. As we go through each soil from this story, examine your own heart and decide which soil your heart is most like.

1. Path Soil

Q: What comes to mind when you think of a path?

Q: What happens to seeds that are scattered on a path?

Q: What kind of heart is Jesus talking about?

Q: What are things that harden a person's heart?
- Hearing the Word, but not doing anything about it
- Being skeptical, analytical and doing nothing
- Deliberately rejecting what you know to be right

2. Rocky Soil

Q: Why would the seed on the rocky soil spring up quickly?
- It is talking about a thin layer of soil over a solid rock base
- Like planting sod on a parking lot

Q: Verse 21 says it has no root. Why would that make a plant wither and die?
- No nourishment system in place

Q: What kind of heart is Jesus referring to?
- Shallow, superficial, emotional
- Likes the idea of following Jesus, but didn't count the cost

Q: Have you ever made an emotional decision? When?

Q: Why do people make emotional decisions?

Q: Verse 21 talks of trouble and persecution. How does this test the roots?

Q: What forms of trouble and persecution come when you become a disciple?
- People attack us, persecution from family, friends, workmates, pressure from society to conform, etc.

Jesus wants us to make a solid decision and sink our roots down deep.

3. Thorny Soil

Q: Why do weeds choke out the garden plants?
- They take all the good nutrition away from the plant.

Q: Describe how weeds can take over a garden.
- Start small, almost unnoticeable
- In a short amount of time, they can take over an entire garden

Q: What are the weeds in life that can choke out God?
- Career, kids, hobbies, money, sports
- Almost anything can replace our love for God if we let it

Q: Are these things bad? No!
Q: How do these things make you unfruitful?
- Distract you, take up all your time, spend time on worthless pursuits

Q: What kind of heart is Jesus talking about?
- A heart not distracted by the cares and worries of the world

4. Good Soil

Q: What kind of heart is Jesus talking about?

Q: What are ways that we can cultivate a good heart?

Q: How can you be fruitful thirty or sixty or one hundred times?

Everyone falls into one of these categories:
1. You are hard toward God's word.
2. You are excited about what you hear, but don't have deep convictions.
3. You have great intentions, but let many things distract you.
4. You have a great heart, are focused and are making disciples.

We all fall into one of these type of soils, one is good and the other three need work.

Search your heart, which soil are you? ʾ

Q: When it comes down to it, who is responsible for your heart?
- You are. You decide what kind of heart you will have.

Decide to be the good soil.
Start being soft and receptive to God's word.
Decide to put down deep roots and to study and pray every day.
Don't let life's activities distract you from God's work.
Cultivate the soil of your heart to be useful to God.

Nebuchadnezzar's Dream

OPENER Q: Describe the wildest/weirdest dream you have ever had.

In tonight's Bible discussion, we are going to look at a dream that a king had that was an incredible dream of prophecy.

Background: Daniel was written about 600 BC; Israel had been conquered and many of its people taken into captivity to Babylon. A number of the young Jewish men of exceptional qualities had been chosen to serve in King Nebuchadnezzar's palace. One of these exceptional men was Daniel.

Daniel 2:1-9   Have the group recap what happens in these verses.

Daniel 2:10-13   Have the group recap what happens in these verses.

Daniel 2:14-23   Have the group recap what happens in these verses.

Daniel 2:24-28   Have the group recap what happens in these verses.

Q: What do you think of Daniel's character so far?
- Humble–Gives God all the credit

Daniel 2:29-35   Have the group recap what happens in these verses.

Daniel 2:36-38   Have the group recap what happens in these verses.

Q: What kingdom is the head of gold?
- Babylonian empire

Daniel 2:39-43   Have the group recap what happens in these verses.

Q: What kingdom came after the Babylonian empire?
- Medo-Persian empire (Medes and the Persians–Iran and Iraq)

Q: What kingdom came after the Medo-Persian empire?
- Greek empire

Q: What kingdom came after the Greek empire?
- Roman empire

Q: If you remember your history, what were some of the reasons that the Roman empire fell?
- They were never totally united, and they eventually crumbled. Rome conquered all the nations around them, yet none of them ever became "Roman." They all hated the Romans and wanted them out, so the Roman empire crumbled because of a lack of unity.

Q: What do you think of the description in verses 40-43?
- Incredible! It was written over seven hundred years before the fall of the Roman empire.

It was during this time period that something incredible occurred.

Daniel 2:44-45 Recap.

Q: What was established during this time period?
- God's kingdom

Q: What are some characteristics of this kingdom?
- It will never be destroyed.
- It will endure forever!

Q: If you asked people what the kingdom of God is, what would they say?
- Heaven
- A period of time when Jesus ruled on the earth
- The earth
- The church

Q: Based on the scriptures we've read, which answer seems to fit?
- The New Testament church

God had the church in mind seven hundred years before it arrived.
God has been dreaming and planning the church for centuries.

Q: What does this tell you about what God thinks about the church?
- He had a great plan for it; it was not an afterthought.

- Be excited about God's church. It isn't just a church; it's the kingdom of God.
- Be excited about the accuracy of the Bible. It perfectly described the political problems leading to the downfall of the Roman empire hundreds of years before it happened.
- Ask someone to study what the kingdom of God is all about with you!

Bible Talk #41 — Faith of a Sick Woman

OPENER   **Q: Has everything gone perfectly in your life?**

Q: What have you had go wrong in your life?

Lesson Scripture

Mark 5:21-34 Recap. Then reread vv24a-26.

Q: What would your attitude toward life be if you had gone through years of sickness like the woman had gone through?
- Negative, cynical, skeptical, bitter, depressed, angry, hopeless

Q: What kind of attitude might this woman have had toward a faith healer? Why?

This was a woman of incredible faith:
- Suffered a lot over a long period of time
- Had gone to many doctors
- Had lost all her money
- Had gotten worse

It almost seems natural and justifiable to be bitter and negative, and to want to give up.

Reread verses 27-28.
She had an incredible reaction to the news of Jesus.

Q: What could have been her reaction?
- "Right...another faith healer, another fake, another trip to town"
- "I wonder how much he'll charge"

Her faith would seem great if this was her first attempt at being healed. How much more incredible this is considering what she had gone through!

Q: What did the woman see that was different about Jesus?
- He didn't charge, and he was successful.
- He loved people. He was on his way to heal Jairus' daughter.

Reread verse 29.
Where others had failed, Jesus healed her and freed her from her suffering.

We are a lot like this woman, searching for healing.
We're looking for love, fulfillment, hope, meaning, purpose, joy, and freedom.
We've spent of lot of time, energy and money looking for the cure.
We look for relief in all the wrong places.

Q: How do we do that?
- Drugs and alcohol
- Relationships
- Sports, hobbies, careers

- False religion
- Materialism

Q: What obstacles did this woman have to overcome to get to Jesus?
- The crowd
- Her own fears, doubts, skepticism
- Her illness
- Fear of rejection by Jesus
- Fear of failing

Q: What obstacles do we face to get to Jesus?
- Laziness
- Lack of time
- Lack of initiative
- Doubts, fears, skepticism

Are you like this great woman of faith?
Are you an overcomer like her?
Are you tough and tenacious and determined, or are you a wimp?
What kind of effort are you making to get closer to Jesus?
What kind of effort are you making to study the Bible?
What kind of effort are you making to get close to spiritual men and women?
What kind of effort are you making to pray and to worship God?

Hundreds of people were smashing against Jesus (like a crowd at a concert or a football game before the gates open) and touching him.

Q: What was different about this woman's touch?
- It wasn't just an accidental touch; it was a touch of faith.

Jesus knew that power had gone out from him.

Many religious people in America go to church and "bump into" Jesus, but their lives are not changed. They are not different afterward.

It's the touch of faith that makes a difference. It changes you!

- Have the faith of the sick woman.
- Forget the past and the disappointments, bag the excuses and the failures.
- Start making an effort to get close to Jesus!

Bible Talk #42

The Ten Virgins

 Q: Have you ever procrastinated on anything?

Q: What are the causes of procrastination?

Q: What are the results of procrastination?

Lesson Scripture

The setting is a discussion of the return of Jesus.

Matthew 24:1-13 Recap.

Q: What did the ten virgins have in common?
- All invited to the banquet
- All knew that the bridegroom would return
- All had made some preparations

Today we have things in common in a religious sense:
- Christian nation
- Belief in God
- Belief in Jesus' return
- Involved in a religious group

Q: How were the virgins foolish?
- No oil, not prepared

Q: How are we unprepared?
- Low level of commitment
- Low knowledge of the Word
- Comfortable, content

Q: What is our example here?
- Jesus–serving, sacrificing, self-denial
- The foolish virgins believed, but they didn't hold to it. (**John 8:31-32**)

Q: How were the wise virgins wise?
- They were prepared.

Q: How were they prepared?
- Anticipated needs
- Knew what was expected

Q: How does God expect us to use this parable?
- To get and stay prepared
- To stay on the edge spiritually, always ready for his return

Q: If Jesus came today, what would he say?
- If we're not ready, he will say "I don't know you."

Q: What is the significance of the midnight arrival?
- No one was expecting it.

Q: Are people sleeping today? How?
- Putting things off, not dealing with sin
- Not searching, not earnestly seeking
- Going with the flow

Q: Are most people going to be ready, and be saved?
- According to **Matthew 7:13,** many are going the broad way that leads to destruction.
- Too many are sleeping and not making adequate preparation.

Q: What things can interfere with your preparation?
- Not urgent/think there is more than enough time
- Fooled into thinking that Jesus is not really hardline about preparation

Read **2 Peter 3:8-9.** Recap.

Q: What does it mean when it says the Lord is not slow in keeping his promises?
- It may seem slow to us, but only because we don't understand the nature of time.
- We don't realize that he is being patient with us.

We must wake up and get prepared. Jesus will return. He will take only those who have been preparing for his return.

Traditions

 Q: What is your favorite holiday? Why?

Q: What are some things we traditionally do on holidays?
- Presents on birthdays
- Turkey/football on Thanksgiving or Christmas
- Love notes/chocolate on Valentine's Day

Q: Is there anything wrong with these traditions?
- Nothing–They are fun, link us to the past, give us security, bring back memories, unite families, etc.

There are two areas that seem to have a lot of traditions built up around them: Holidays and religion.

Let's look at a time when Jesus had something to say about religious tradition.

 Matthew 15:1-9 Recap.

Q: Why was Jesus so upset about what they were teaching?
- Breaking God's command for the sake of tradition (v3)
- Nullifying God's command for the sake of tradition (v6)
- Worship in vain, teachings are but rules taught by men

When traditions started to get in the way of God's commands, Jesus got upset. Traditions are like practical jokes: some are "nice" or "cute," but some are serious and can be dangerous.

Q: What are some "nice," "cute" religious traditions?
- Nice clothes on Sunday
- Meet in buildings with stained glass and steeple
- Worship on Sunday morning
- Order of worship service
- Sunday evening service
- Robes on clergy
- Prayer before meals

You could go on for hours...

Q: What are some dangerous traditions that are not taught in the Bible?
- Jesus yes, church no (i.e. I can be tight with Jesus without going to church)
- Many denominations–Bible teaches that there is one church
- Infant Baptism–It is never mentioned in the Bible
- Confirmation–Word isn't found in the Bible, practice never mentioned
- Praying Jesus into your heart–No one in the Bible ever did it, never taught anywhere in the Scriptures
- Once saved, always saved–Another false tradition found nowhere in the Scriptures

I'm sure I stepped on just about everyone's toes, but it is important to stop and ask why you believe what you do.

Is it Biblical? Or is it tradition?

Reread verses 8-9.

Q: What is the real issue with traditions?
- Jesus isn't Lord. We are doing what we want, not what he wants.
- God doesn't have your heart. (If you love me, you will obey me.)

Q: Why is it so hard to break free of tradition?
- Parents and family
- Emotional ties
- Link to the past
- It is what you've been taught to believe in
- Momentum
- Pride–I don't want to be wrong, to look bad, to look stupid

All of us at one time or another have had notions or ideas about God, about Jesus and worship, about heaven and about salvation that were wrong.

Q: If we don't break free of traditions, what is the alternative?
- Our hearts end up far from God. (vv8-9)
- We end up in vain worship.

Read **John 8:31-32.**

Q: What does this verse say it takes to be a true disciple?
- Hold tightly to Jesus' teaching
- Follow Jesus' teaching–not traditions, not what people say, not our feelings, not what we have always been taught, not what we want to believe, not what religious leaders say, not what our family says

Challenge your traditions! Ask why. Is it true?
Where does the Bible teach that? When was that first taught?
Did anyone in the Bible do it that way?
Rely on God's word, not on tradition.

Thanks into Action

OPENER Use your imagination and let's have some fun: You are in debt for $20 million to Donald Trump, and you can't declare bankruptcy.

Q: How did you get into debt for $20 million?

Q: How do you feel being so deeply in debt?

Q: Have you ever had any kind of debt forgiven? How did it feel?

Let's look at a parable that Jesus told about a couple of people who had debts forgiven.

Lesson Scripture

Matthew 18:21-35 Recap.

Q: How much was ten thousand talents of silver worth?
- It was worth approximately $74 millon.

Q: Why did Jesus use ten thousand talents to illustrate the first guy's debt?
- To show he had a lot of debt

Q: How would you feel if you owed $74 millon with no hope to repay?

Q: How would you feel to have the debt forgiven?
- Grateful, thankful, relieved

Q: Who knows how much one hundred denarii is worth?
- About seventeen dollars–not much

Q: In this story, who is the rich king?
- God

Q: Who owes the ten thousand talents?
- You and me

Q: Do you owe anything to God?

Q: If he billed you for services rendered, what would you owe to God?
- Spouse, children, eyesight, health, friends, mental abilities, forgiveness, peace joy, love, etc.

Q: Has God ever billed you for these things?

Q: Verse 25 says that the guy and his family were about to be sold. Does this seem fair to you?
- Of course–the debt was legally enforcable. Justice would be served.

The good news is that the master was merciful, not only "just."

Q: What would be fair for God to collect from you?
- Anything and everything–We owe God an incredible debt with no way to even begin paying him.

Q: Has God ever billed you?
- No way
- God has forgiven our debts. He writes "Paid in Full" on the bill.

Q: How should this servant have reacted?
- Joyful, thankful, excited

Q: Was this servant thankful? How do you know?
- This servant was totally selfish.
- He didn't even consider how much he had been forgiven. He was ungrateful, unthankful and abusive.

Q: How are we like the ungrateful servant?
- Unforgiving with our spouse/roommate, when we have been forgiven a lot
- Unloving toward others, when we have been loved a lot
- Unthankful toward God, when he has given us so much
- Intolerant of others' quirks, when others are so tolerant of our faults
- Impatient with others, when others are so patient with us
- Don't share how much we have been given/forgiven
- Aren't joyful or excited about the incredible gifts God has given us

Q: How does God feel about ungratefulness?
- He hates it (vv32-35).

Q: How can we not be like the ungrateful servant?
- Be aware of how much God has blessed our lives.
- Don't be ignorant of God's blessings.
- Share how much God has done for you.
- Stop being critical, negative and complaining about what you don't have.
- Be tolerant, forgiving and patient with the people around you.

Thankfulness isn't just a state of mind, it is putting it into action.
When you are a thankful person, it shows up in the way you treat others.

Spend some time this week telling God what you are thankful for in your life. Put your thankfulness into action in the way you treat others.

Bible Talk #45

Hope

 Q: What is one thing that you hoped for as a kid? A dream?

Hope is what gives us the strength to go on and tackle the future. We're going to discuss what the Bible says about hope.

Q: What are some things we hope for?
- Success in career
- Success in sports, hobbies
- School
- Girlfriend/wife

Q: Looking at the world, does the world have a lot of hope in it?
- Marriage/divorces as bad as ever
- Corruption in government/immorality
- AIDS/STD rampant

The Bible holds out a hope that lasts.

 1 Peter 1:3-9 Recap.

Q: What kind of hope are we talking about?

Q: What does this hope produce?
- Inexpressible, glorious joy
- Knowing we have received the goal
- Purpose
- Eternal relationship with God
- Salvation

This is exciting!

Remember back on the greatest things we hoped for.

Q: What did we have to do to receive/accomplish them?
- Cost something
- Money
- Time
- Pride/effort
- Break off or change relationships
- Plans, dreams, goals, aspirations

We were willing to give up something to get something better.

In order to have the hope of that relationship with God, it will cost us something.

Luke 14:33 says it will cost everything to be a disciple of Jesus.

Q: What will it cost you?
- Your pride
- Your sin
- Your goals, dreams, plans
- Your desire to be in control

Q: But what will you gain?
- Jesus, and that is the ultimate that anyone can gain! We then have a living hope!

 Make a decision to have the hope that cannot be diminished or taken away.

Bible Talk #46

Beauty and the Beast

 OPENER   Discuss the movie *Beauty and the Beast.*

Q: Under what circumstances are you "the Beauty"? When are you "the Beast"?

Q: What is something your mate does for you that makes you feel special?
- God wants our marriages to be special, fantastic, hot!

Don't have people turn to the references but discuss the following scriptures:
- **Proverbs 18:22**–He who finds a wife, finds what is good.
- **Deuteronomy 24:5**–Men are to stay home from war for a year to make their wives happy.
- **Genesis 2:18-25**–God designed and planned for marriage.

Q: Why do marriages fall apart?
- Poor communication, selfishness, fall out of love, no time together
- Basically it is a lack of unity, God wants us to be totally unified

Genesis 2:24–They became one.

Tonight we will be discussing the roles of husbands and wives.

 Main Point   God gives the roles. When we try to change them, confusion reigns. He teaches men and women what they need to do to make a great marriage.

Q: Why does God have different roles for husbands and wives?
- To preserve unity

Let's see what God says are some roles for husband and wife.

Read **Ephesians 5:22-33.**

Let's talk about the role of the wife first:
Read verse 24. Wives are to submit to their husbands in everything.
We attach (incorrectly) bad connotations to the word "submit." It might be more accurate to think of it as "adapting" to husbands in everything.

Let's talk about submission by defining what it is not:

Q: What doesn't submission mean?
- That it is just for women (**Ephesians 5:21**)
- Slavery, inferiority
- Never opening your mouth, giving suggestions or giving advice
- Suppressed, folded up, hiding abilities, stepped on, dominated, wimpy

Look at submission the way God looks at it:

1. The wife must make herself submissive, the husband can't force it.

2. Submission is spiritual, it is commanded by God.
3. It emphasizes the "shoulds" and not the "should-nots."
4. It includes attitudes as well as actions.

Q: Why does it include attitudes as well as actions?
- Submitting or adapting to the husband is not to weaken the wife, but to strengthen the marriage.

Q: Why does the Bible say to submit or adapt in everything?
- If we pick and choose, we really won't be unified.

Q: What makes it hard to submit to someone?

The Bible says the husband is the head of the wife as Christ is the head of the church:

Q: What would happen if we did not submit to Christ?
- Disunity with God, same in marriage

Husbands are commanded to be the leader and the lover. (vv22-25)

Q: How did Christ lead? What did he lead in?
- By example in submissiveness to God, meeting people's needs, loving unconditionally, in humility (considering others better), sacrifice, etc.

Q: How responsible is a husband for his wife and his marriage?
- Totally! If there is something in your mate that you don't like, then ask, "What do I need to put to death in me in order to change my spouse."

Q: What can a husband do to change things in the home like a frantic lifestyle, pride, lack of communication, disobedient children, etc?
- Leading by example, sacrificing, denying themselves, loving the most, saying "I'm sorry" first, making up first, giving in first, etc.

Q: Men: How would you feel if your mate was submissive in the way the Bible says?
- Great, fun, easy to lead, inspired, secure, easy to love

Q: Women: How would you feel if your husband was as loving and sacrifical as Jesus was with the church?
- Happy, loved, secure, easy to follow, easy to submit

 Conclusion God's plan works! We must study the Bible and apply it to our lives and marriages.

Bible Talk #47

Open Communication

 Have everyone take a sheet of paper and answer the following:

1. What was the date of your wedding?
2. What was the time of day and day of the week?
3. What color were the bridesmaids' dresses?
4. Where did you go on your first date?

Have each couple share their answers together, and have fun!

Q: What things in a marriage need to be communicated?
- Schedule, feelings, attitudes, expectations, discipline of kids, dreams, desires plans, fears, concerns, etc.

Q: Why is communication so important?
- Unity, conflict resolution, so you can meet each other's needs

Q: What are some things in human nature that can be a barrier to good communication?
- Insensitivity, selfishness, self-centeredness, arrogance, fear of rejection, resentments, attitudes, etc.

Let's look at four aspects of good communication:

1. Being outwardly expressive

Luke 6:43-45– "Out of the overflow of his heart..."

Q: Generally speaking, how do men's and women's communication differ?
- Men give the facts, shorter and to the point, hard to communicate feelings
- Women share feelings, more and longer, more expressive

Q: Why is it important in a marriage for you to be expressive?
- Communication brings intimacy and unity
- Unexpressed feelings turn into bad attitudes
- It reveals your heart...where the heart is, actions follow
- It is the key to helping each other be right with God

2. Having pride-killing humility

Philippians 2:1-3–"Consider others better than yourselves."

Q: How does pride kill good communication?
- Pride wants to get its point across, and doesn't listen to the other person.
- Pride is not willing to be vulnerable or close.

Q: How can we have the humility we need for good communication?
- See yourself as you are without God.
- Truly see your spouse as better than yourself.
- Confess sin regularly.
- Pray for humility and be unified with your spouse.

3. Being expressively respectful

Ephesians 5:33–The "wife must respect her husband."
1 Peter 3:7–The husband must respect his wife.

Q: Why is respect so critical to good communication?

Q: How do you feel when you are disrespected?

Q: What are some ways to show and express your respect for your mate?
- Note: God doesn't say your mate must earn respect! It is commanded.

4. Nothing is more important than your relationship with God and his son, Jesus.

Luke 14:25-26–Must hate father, brother, husband, wife...

Q: What does this scripture mean?
- Jesus comes first in your life, above all relationships.

Q: How does making Jesus our Lord help us in our communication?
- Teaches us to love others first, and to put their needs first above our own
- A great disciple can learn, grow and change

Q: What happens when something or someone else is more important than God?
- We won't have the right standard.
- We will do what we want, when we want, how we want.
- We will compromise our marriage, our children and ourselves.

This teaching is so contrary to what we learn from society:
- Learn to get your point across, not how to meet spouse's needs
- Communication is for selfish reasons, not for unity
- Look out for number one, not submissive
- Pride–never show a weakness, no humility, no consideration for others

These things are the by-products of being a disciple of Jesus.
The key to great communication is to change yourself.
The way to do that is to continually make decisions to be like Jesus.

O–Outwardly expressive
P–Pride-killing humility
E–Expressively respectful
N–Nothing before God/Jesus

 Put it into practice!

Resolving Conflict

OPENER Q: What is the dumbest thing you and your spouse ever argued about?

Q: What are some typical things that couples have conflict over?
• Money, house, kids, jobs, sex...you name it!

Q: What does unresolved conflict do?
• Creates resentments, destroys intimacy, causes disunity

Q: How does unresolved conflict come out? How does it show itself?
• Yelling, kicking the dog, sarcasm, ignoring the other person, silence

Q: Does the lack of an argument mean that a conflict doesn't exist?
• No—It probably means there isn't open communication.

Conflict is inevitable because everyone is unique and has different opinions, different needs, different tastes, different likes and dislikes.

James 4:1-3 (Source of quarrels) Recap.

Q: What keeps us from resolving conflict?
• Selfish desires, selfish motives, not living to please God

Ephesians 4:1-3 (Be completely humble) Recap.

Q: What does God say needs to be our attitude to keep unity in the marriage?
• Complete humility, not selective humility
• Bearing with one another, patient (like Jesus is with us)
• Presume that your mate is innocent!

Ephesians 4:17-5:2 (Godly living) Recap.
Let's look at some practical ways to avoid conflict in our marriages.

Q: In verse 18, of what are these people ignorant?
• How to live a godly (happy, joyful) life

Q: Why are they ignorant?
• Given into their own desires (sin), and their hearts are hardened

Q: Are we naturally good at resolving conflict (think of a two-year-old)?

Q: What do verses 22-24 say about how to become good at resolving conflict?
• Need to be taught, need to learn it, everyone can learn to be better

Q: Verse 25 says, "speak truthfully." How does that avoid conflict?
- Exaggeration adds fuel to the fire
- e.g."He always..," "She never...,"

Q: What does verse 26 mean, "In your anger do not sin"?
- Don't let your emotions run away with you, making things worse.

Q: Why is it a good idea to resolve conflicts the same day?
- Means you will be angry less time
- Keeps Satan from using your situation to hurt you
- Frees you up to serve and love the next day

Q: What does verse 29 have to do with resolving conflict?
- Don't say anything in an argument that is mean and spiteful.
- Discuss the point of disagreement; don't bring in other issues.
- Don't call names or cut down your mate.
- Don't argue in front of your children. (It makes them insecure.)

Q: Read verse 32. How does God forgive you?
- Totally, forgets it ever happened, never brings it up again
- Loves even when you aren't sorry for what you did

Q: How should we forgive our mate?
- The same way!

Read **Ephesians 5:1-2.**

Q: How would we do at resolving conflict if we imitated God?

Here is a little personal test for you to answer to yourself:
- Is your attitude that your spouse is better than you? Are you completely humble and gentle?
- Do you forgive like God forgives you?
- Do you only say what builds up and benefits your mate?
- Do you speak the truth to your mate (no exaggeration)?
- Are you striving to imitate God?

Q: How well do you think most people you know would do on this test?
- There is a big difference between an average marriage and a great marriage. The study tonight was not aimed at making you more religious, it was aimed at helping you to be right with God and resolve conflicts God's way.

 Read the Bible and find out what God says about having a great marriage!

Romance in Marriage

Bible Talk #49

OPENER Q: What would be your dream date with your spouse?

Q: What are things your spouse wants in a romantic evening?

Q: What are things you want in a romantic evening?
- Identify the differences

Q: Why are there differences?
- We are different and have different ideas and expectations.
- Reference *My Fair Lady*–"Why can't a woman be more like a man?"

Need: To love your mate
To love is to give what is needed–Not what you want, but what they need.

Q: Women: What are some words that you think of when you think of romance?
- Courtship, adventure, excitement, respect, tenderness, candlelight, flowers, quiet walks, anticipation, devotion, caress, embrace, etc.

Q: Women: How do you feel when those ideas are expressed/conveyed by your husband?
- Warm, radiant, confident, feminine, secure, etc.

Read **Ephesians 5:25-27.**

Q: Men: In view of Ephesians 5:25-27, what is your response?
- Love your wife unselfishly, give her what she needs

Q: How do you know if you are loving your wife the way Christ loves the church?
- Look at your wife–Is she radiant?

Read **Acts 20:35.** "It is more blessed to give than to receive."

Q: Men: In view of Acts 20:35, what will be the result?
- Blessed!

Q: How?
- Happy, joyful, radiant wife
- You will be a happy man
- You feel great because you gave

Loving your wife and meeting her needs is a "wise investment."

Q: Men: What are some things you think of when you think of romance?
- Sex, beautiful scenery, dinner out, movie

Women's understanding in general of romance is broader than the understanding many men have. Many men have a tendency toward selfishness and insensitivity in this area, and need to be trained to view romance differently.

Read **Ephesians 5:1-2.**
1. Imitate God by living a life of love.
2. Christ loved the church and gave himself up for it.

Q: In the context of romance, what does it mean to give yourselves up for your wives?
- To do what they want, to meet their needs

3. It takes sacrifice, giving up what you want to do.

Note that **Ephesians 5:28** says to love your wives like you love yourselves.

To be imitators of God, we need to learn of God's character and to practice his behavior. That's where discipling comes in. Husbands need to be trained to "love" by other men who have been trained. (**Matthew 28:18-20**)

 Romance is whatever your mate thinks it is.
We are privileged to give to our mates.
We need to learn to be romantic.
The Bible contains the principles for marriage.
The benefits of our efforts are tremendous.
We will enjoy the promises of **Proverbs 5:18-19.**
Homework: Read Song of Solomon together (Alone)!

A Great Marriage

 Activity Newlywed Game: Give each couple a piece of paper and a pencil. (No one need leave the room.) Have one spouse write an answer, then have the other spouse respond verbally. Then compare the answers:

1) Wives: What is your dream career?
2) Husbands: What is the last dish that your wife made that you didn't like?
3) Wives: When was the last time the two of you went on an awesome date?
4) Husbands: What was your last bump about and who caused it?

Have some fun with this and enjoy the answers.

Q: What do most people expect out of marriage?
- Some fun, a companion, some laughs, a friend for a while
- A few kids, and sooner or later, a divorce

Most people don't have very high expectations for marriage.

Q: What picture of marriage is painted by movies and television?
- Divorces, unfaithfulness, unhappiness, abuse, nagging, unsubmissive wives, abusive husbands, lousy lovers, boring sex

I've got great news. God has a great plan for your marriage!
God has incredibly high expectations for your marriage!

1. **Genesis 1:26-27**–You are created special.

Q: What do you notice about how God created people?
- In his image!

Q: What attributes does God have that we also have?
- Feelings, emotions, sense of humor, capacity to love, senses, etc.

You were created special, not just as an evolved animal. You are like God!
You need to feel great about yourself and your mate!

2. **Genesis 2:18-23**–Your mate is a gift from God.

Q: What do you own that is valuable? How do you demonstrate its value?

Notice that Eve was a gift from God!
You need to see your spouse as a special gift from God.
How incredibly valuable is a gift from God, the creator of the universe.
Care for it, protect, treasure it, talk about it.

3. **Ephesians 5:21-33**–Three keys to an awesome marriage:

A. "Submit to one another out of reverence for Christ." (v21)

Q: What does it mean to submit?
- Voluntarily place yourself under someone else

Q: Who is called to submit?
- Everyone

Q: Why should we submit?
- Without it, there is strife and animosity
- It is a way of giving, showing humility, is Christ-like

Q: What keeps us from submitting?
- Pride and arrogance

B. "Husbands, love your wives, just as Christ loved the church and gave himself up for her..." (v25)

Q: Why are husbands told to love their wives?
- We can be pretty unloving at times.

Q: How did Christ love the church?
- Worked hard to establish it, suffered for it, died for it

Q: What does it mean to give yourself up for your wife?
- Put her needs first before your own, look out for her first, etc.

Q: How would most wives feel if their husbands loved them this way?

C. Wives, submit to and respect your husbands. (vv22 and 33)

Q: Why specifically are wives called to submit?

Q: Is submission conditional?
- e.g. "If he does this, then I will..."

Q: What does it mean to respect your husband?

Q: Describe what happens when these three things are put into practice.

Q: What keeps us from putting these things into practice?
- Want the other to go first
- Make the spouse earn our love, respect, submission
- Faithless–it won't work, skeptical, "They'll never change"
- Pride, selfishness, laziness–it's hard work!
- Want control, want to manipulate spouse
- Focused on the other's faults, blind to our own sin

Q: What's the measure of what kind of husband/wife you are?
- Look at your mate
- Is your wife radiant? Joyful? Secure? Is your husband confident and secure?

 Trust God's way! God has a great plan for your marriage! Don't give in to fear. You put it into practice–don't wait on your mate. Get another couple involved in your marriage to get an objective viewpoint.

God Is Not Like Us

 OPENER Have you ever considered what it would be like if everyone was just like you? Looked like you, smiled like you, laughed like you, talked like you, had your sense of humor, acted and reacted like you?

Q: What do you think the world would be like?

What if God was just like you? Acted like you? Loved like you? Forgave like you? Was merciful like you? Was unselfish like you? Gave like you?

Q: How would you like that?

Good News! God is not just like us!

Q: What are some common images we have of God? Where do we get these images?
- Parents, grandpas, preachers, television, movies, etc.

 Lesson Scripture **Read Luke 15:11-32** Recap.

Called the Parable of the Prodigal Son, but it is really about our Father! Let's look at three aspects of our Father that are unlike us.

1. God gives us freedom (vv11-13).

Q: How did the son want his freedom?
- Wanted his inheritance early, wanted to move out and take his money

Q: Do you think the father tried to talk him out of it? Could the father have stopped him?
- Yes!

Q: What did the father do?
- Let him leave

Q: What might some of our responses have been if we were in the father's shoes?
- Want to control or restrict
- Don't want people to make bad choices or get hurt
- Get angry or jealous

Aren't you glad God is not like us?
God gives us the freedom–even the freedom to blow it.:
- To do good or to do evil, to sin or not to sin
- To love your neighbor, or not to love your neighbor
- To have a great marriage, or a mediocre one
- To have a great relationship with God, or to ignore him

Freedom is powerful yet frightening, because with freedom comes responsibility. Sometimes people who are given freedom make bad choices and blow it.

Q: How did the son blow it?
- Squandered all his money, lived a wild and sinful life, became a pig herder, ate with the pigs, lost all his friends, humiliated himself

But then something incredible happened, etc....(v17), he came to his senses.

2. God is compassionate. (v20)

Q: How was the father compassionate?
- Saw him from a long way off (looking for him), filled with compassion
- Ran to his son, threw his arms around him and kissed him

Q: What are some ways we might respond in this situation?
- I told you so. You blew it. What do you want?
- Give a clammy reception, make him grovel and beg
- Make him know how much he hurt you, what sins he was involved in

The son hurt the father badly, but look at how the father responded.

Q: How do you respond when you are hurt?

Aren't you glad that God is not like us? Most of us are out of touch with what God is really like!

3. God is forgiving (vv21-24).

Q: How did the father treat the son after his initial greeting?
- Threw a party

Q: What does this show about the father's heart?
- Thankful, overjoyed, forgiving

Q: If you were the father, how would v21 read?
- Then the father said to the son: "You are no longer worthy to be my son."
- What exactly did you do in the far country?
- When and how are you going to pay me back?
- Do you have any idea how much grief you've caused me and this family?

When God forgives, he forgives completely, fully, totally!
He doesn't bring it up anymore and he doesn't rub your nose in it.
Aren't you glad God is not like us?

 Conclusion
I hope this study has given you a clearer picture of God. Don't let preconceived ideas about God keep you from the truth about his love for each of us.
Dig into the Bible to find out what God is really like.
Be encouraged...God is not like us!

Bible Talk #52

Build on the Solid Rock

 OPENER   Imagine you absolutely knew you were going to be hit by a storm exactly one month from now. How would you prepare your home?

In each of our lives we will experience trauma, trials, tribulations and stress. Some are expected and some are unexpected–death of friends, loved ones, births, moving, illness, etc. Some are totally unexpected and come without any advance warning. Jesus talked about preparing for the storms of life in the Sermon on the Mount.

 Lesson Scripture   Read **Luke 6:46-49.** Recap.

Q: Which of the two houses were easier to build? Why?
- It is easier to build a foundation on sand than on rock.

Q: Which house looked stronger?
- You could not tell from the outside.

Q: Why would anyone build a house on a weak foundation?
- It's easier, it's cheaper, it's faster.
- They didn't actually have to live there.
- They didn't think they would ever get a storm.

Jesus told this parable to paint a spiritual picture for us to think about.

Q: What does the house represent?
- Your life before God

Q: What does it mean, "its destruction was complete"?
- Lost their faith, life falls apart, lost hope for the future and a reason to live

Q: What are the floods and torrents in people's lives?
- Disease, drugs, addictions, alcoholism
- Financial disaster, losing a job, not getting a promotion
- Losing a loved one, parent, child, friend
- Broken relationships, divorce, unfaithfulness of a spouse
- Physical trauma, accidents and much, much more

Q: How bad are the storms in your life going to be?
- No one in this world knows.

Maybe your life will be a bed of roses, but maybe not.
Some of you are out of touch and think "It'll never happen to me."
How will you weather the storms of life?
How will your faith in God hold out?

Q: What does it mean to have a foundation on the rock?
- Faith in God, trust in God

Q: How much faith?
- So much that it will weather any storm

Q: What is the difference between the two builders?
- Both heard the Word
- One obeyed and the other ignored it

Q: What does it take to dig down deep?
- Must be convinced that the storms are coming and that they will test your faith
- Got to have faith that Jesus is the right foundation to build on
- Got to have perseverance to keep on digging
- Got to put into practice what you know

Some of us are trying to build a foundation with a trowel or a screwdriver!
- You read a few verses a day.
- You pray about three minutes a day.
- You have shallow convictions about who Jesus really is.
- You have shallow convictions about the Bible and the kingdom of God.

Some of us think we are a match for the storms of life and what will come.
- We must not be naive.
- We must dig down deep.
- We must build on the solid rock.

God wants everyone to be able to weather the storms of life.
God wants all of us to end up in heaven with him.

- Get into the Word. Study it every day to see how God wants us to live.
- Hear the word of God–then put it into practice.
- Spend time every day in prayer. Develop a great walk with God.

Invitation Samples

It's important to be creative when doing a Bible talk series. These samples show different ideas that can be used. Try to use concepts that meet felt needs, hot topics of the day, etc.

Interested in learning more about the Bible?
Please be our guest for the area

Bible Talk

● Informal setting   ● Friendly atmosphere
● Discover Genuine Christianity!

Take the opportunity to be a part of something
that can really change your life!

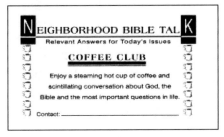

NEIGHBORHOOD BIBLE TALK

Relevant Answers for Today's Issues

COFFEE CLUB

Enjoy a steaming hot cup of coffee and
scintillating conversation about God, the
Bible and the most important questions in life.

Contact: _____

Dinner & **A Bible Talk**

Enjoy a delicious meal and an informal discussion
about Life, the Bible, and how God has the
answers for all of the many challenges we face.

Contact _____

Always and Forever!

Always and Forever!

In an age of boring marriages, troubled marriages, and divorce, family psychologists and experts agree that every marriage needs a time of revitalization. Even good marriages need to grow. "Always and Forever" is a special marriage seminar designed to make your marriage indestructible.

"Always and Forever" will be held at the Winn Brook School in Belmont.

April 21 . . . . "A Romantic Meal" . . . . 6:30 p.m.
6:15 p.m. . . . . "The Way We Were"
May 4, 7:30 p.m. . . . . "Thats What I Like about You"
May 11, 7:30 . . . . "Solid As a Rock"

We have prepared a special meal for couples at this first meeting at a cost of $10.00 per couple.

R.S.V.P. ....

Phone: ....

Sponsored by: Boston Church of Christ

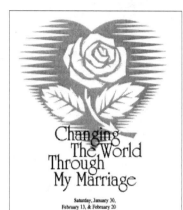

Changing The World Through My Marriage

Saturday, January 30,
February 13, & February 20

Great Performances
Marriage & Family Enrichment

Most of us love to go to the movies. We have chosen movie titles to highlight the topics of an inspiring series of Bible-centered discussions designed to meet our needs for a great marriage and family life.

Week 1	**Places in the Heart** ...God's vision for heart to heart relationships
Week 2	**She-Devil** and **The Jerk** ...The problem with us is me!
Week 3	**Look Who's Talking** ...Learning to listen and speak to build up
Week 4	**Dances with Wolves** ...Keeping romance alive
Week 5	**Parenthood** ...The kind of parents who raise happy children
Week 6	**Problem Child** ...Winning obedience & respect from your children

Location ....

Time & Day ....

Invited by ....

Phone ....

LIFE'S CRUCIAL QUESTIONS

October 2 . . . . **Why All The Fuss?**
Wednesday (Catholics vs. Protestants)

October 4 . . . . **"I'm O.K...I think?"**
Friday

Time: 7:30 p.m.

Location: Best Western Hotel
Junction of Route 2 and Route 31

If you are like most people you have many questions concerning God that are difficult to find answers to. This series will address two of the most commonly asked questions and provide biblical answers. Please come and join us for what will be a very informative and enlightening time to answer LIFE'S CRUCIAL QUESTIONS.

Further Info. ....

Sponsored by the Church of Christ

What No Marriage/Family Can Resist

Boring or Exhilarating?—"True Love"
October 12 — 7:30-8:30 p.m.

Friends or Foe?—"What Makes a Strong Marriage"
October 19 — 7:30-8:30 p.m.

Intimate or Distant?—"Let's Talk"
October 26 — 7:30-8:30 p.m.

The Best or Worst?—"What Children Need Most"
November 2 — 7:30-8:30 p.m.

For info _____

What No Marriage/Family Can Resist

H · O · M · E

R eal I ssues
BIBLE DISCUSSION SERIES

Y ou Live, You Die, . . .
Then What?

W hy Philosophy Fails

C hristianity: Why the
Controversy?

W e invite you to join us each week for
BIBLE TALK-- an informal, small-group
discussion of relevant topics. Everyone is
welcome regardless of religious experience
or preference.

Time:
Location:

THE Price of Success

Every man aspires to be successful. It is the dream of some and the reality of others. Whether you are the dreamer or the accomplished, success has its price. You are invited to attend a men's breakfast featuring two speakers who have first hand experience and knowledge of the "Price of Success".

The Two Great Men of Christmas

A special holiday
discussion series

Date:
A Legend and a Lord
—By Mansion and by Manger

Date:
A Giver and a Gift
—By Night and by Might

Date:
A Deliverer and a Deliverance
—By Carriage and by Cross

Date:
A Season and a Savior
—By Appreciation and by Depreciation

Location:

For information: _____

Who Are We?

Discipleship Publications International (DPI) began publishing in 1993. We are a non-profit Christian publisher committed to publishing and distributing materials that honor God, lift up Jesus Christ and show how his message practically applies to all areas of life. We have a deep conviction that no one changes life like Jesus and that the implementation of his teaching will revolutionize any life, any marriage, any family and any singles household.

Since our beginning we have published more than 100 titles; plus we have produced a number of important, spiritual audio products. More than one million volumes have been printed, and our works have been translated into more than a dozen languages—international is not just a part of our name! Our books are shipped monthly to every inhabited continent.

To see a more detailed description of our works, find us on the World Wide Web at **www.dpibooks.org**. You can order books listed on the following pages by calling 1-888-DPI-BOOK 24 hours a day. From outside the US, call 978-670-8840, ext. 227 during Boston-area business hours.

We appreciate the hundreds of comments we have received from readers. We would love to hear from you. Here are other ways to get in touch:

Mail: DPI, 2 Sterling Rd, Billerica, MA 01862-2595
E-mail: dpibooks@icoc.org

Find us on the
World Wide Web

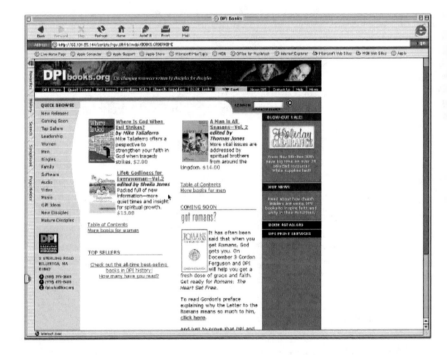

www.dpibooks.org

How to Share Your Faith

With inspiring real–life stories from around the world

BY FRANK AND ERICA KIM

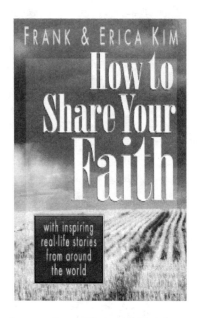

Every disciple wants to lead others to Jesus Christ. This unique book will show you how to do it. And more than that, it will inspire you to do it with joy.

Frank and Erica Kim, leaders of the largest Christian church of any kind in the history of Japan, have written powerful heart-moving chapters on sharing with strangers, loving your family and your neighbors, building great friendships, loving the poor, never giving up, and other vital topics. Linked with each chapter by the Kims are faith-building stories from around the world of disciples who put the Bible's message into practice, and saw the results the Kims describe. The stories of more than a hundred people will show readers just how they, too, can make an eternal difference.

The Promises of God
EDITED BY THOMAS AND SHEILA JONES

The Bible is filled with what Peter calls "great and precious promises" from God. In this book, leaders from around the world examine some of these promises and show how trusting in them gives strength, confidence and calm to our hearts and minds. God has given us his promises to encourage us and give us a reason to never ever give up. This book will give loads of encouragement to those who read it.

The Spirit
The Work of the Holy Spirit in the Lives of Disciples
BY DOUGLAS JACOBY

The Spirit is really two books in one. In Part One Douglas shows in practical ways how to walk in the Spirit and live in the Spirit's power. In Part Two the reader will find a more technical discussion of many issues connected with the Charismatic and Neopentecostal movements of the twentieth century, as well as Biblical answers to a host of other questions. For all of those who want a sound understanding of the living water that Jesus promised (John 7:38), this book will meet many needs.

The Leader's Resource Handbook

A unique collection of materials from a variety of leaders in one handy volume. This material will train, equip, inspire and motivate. Great for those leading small groups as well as for full-time leaders of larger ministries. Spiral-bound.

Letters to New Disciples

BY THOMAS A. JONES

In this book, DPI's editor-in-chief addresses twenty-four vital issues faced by new Christians and helps them see God's plan for winning the battles. The most difficult time for new Christians is in their first few months as a disciple. This book is designed to help them through those early challenges.

Mind Change
The Overcomer's Handbook
(Second Edition–Revised and Expanded)

BY THOMAS A. JONES

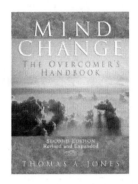

Life is full of challenges: pain, illness, insecurity, sin, confusion and death. None of these surprise God. This book is written to help you see that (1) your challenges are not unusual and (2) God's plan for overcoming will work for you. Thomas Jones writes out of his experience of living with multiple sclerosis and applies what he has learned to overcoming various challenges.

The Killer Within
An African Look at Disease, Sin and Keeping Yourself Saved

BY MIKE TALIAFERRO

What do the Ebola virus, cholera, meningitis and the Guinea worm have to do with sin? In this poignant book you will find out. Mike Taliaferro has done it again! In his unique style he uses the physical world to paint a vivid picture of the deeper, more crucial issue of sin's effect on the soul. Powerful images of disease and sickness drive home the conviction that sin must never be taken lightly.

9 to 5 and Spiritually Alive
Pour Yourself a Fresh Cup of Life
BY SHEILA JONES

Do you work 9 to 5 and sometimes feel "barely alive"? Do you want to be "spiritually alive" and to make an impact on the people around you? Can it be done? Sheila Jones and the women with whom she spoke say, "Absolutely!" And in this new book you hear their reasons.

Drawing on responses from as many as a hundred working women, Sheila gives practical help with a variety of issues faced by women in the workforce.

Friends and Lovers
Marriage As God Designed It
BY SAM AND GERI LAING

Best friends. Exciting lovers. Rarely has the heart and soul of marriage been summed up any better. Friendship and romantic love are the two essential ingredients of a great marriage, the qualities that will make it grow ever richer, deeper and more fulfilling. Many have seen marriage as a drain rather than a fountainhead, a battleground instead of a refuge, and a pit stop rather than a permanent home. This book shows how all that can change.

Some Sat in Darkness
Spiritual Recovery from
Addiction and Codependency
BY MIKE AND BRENDA LEATHERWOOD,
DECLAN JOYCE AND JOANNE RANDALL

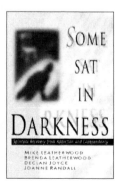

Help for those who have been challenged by addiction and those committed to helping them—a book of hope. Steve Johnson, evangelist in the New York City church, writes: "With God, we have found the most effective way of dealing with drugs in the world."

Spiritual Leadership

A series for leaders and those who want to lead

BY SCOTT AND LYNNE GREEN

Nothing great happens in the kingdom of God on any level without effective leadership. In this series, you will be exposed to God's unique and powerful message about leadership, especially as it is found in the letters of 1 and 2 Timothy.

Included are three dynamic sessions:

SESSION ONE
"Command and Teach":
Who's Charting the Course?
Scott Green

SESSION TWO
"The Worst of Sinners":
The Power of Humility
Scott Green

SESSION THREE
"With Great Patience and Careful Instruction":
How Much Do You Care?
Men: Scott Green   Women: Lynne Green

Some of the comments from those who attended:

    • *The best seminar I have heard since World Missions Seminars in Boston. The church needs these types of dynamic teachings to "reinspire" the movement.*

    • *This has been an incredible three hours. People have told me that I have leadership qualities, but I never knew how to lead. This has helped me a lot.*

    • *Refreshing—a different perspective and ways of looking at leadership. It wasn't the "pat" answers of how to lead, but very real answers. It took into account that people are not robots.*

Scott and Lynne Green have led the China World Sector of the International Churches of Christ since planting the Hong Kong church in 1988. In less than ten years in Hong Kong, they saw the new planting grow to a Sunday attendance of almost three thousand. They have been used by God to raise up dozens of strong and powerful leaders in the kingdom of God and are well qualified to speak on the subject of spiritual leadership. They have two children, Stephen and Ariel.

Walking with God

BY RUSS EWELL

Russ Ewell, one of the most dynamic speakers in the kingdom of God, shows that having a relationship with God is the most exciting thing a human being can do with his life. Topics include (1) Wrestling with God, (2) Walking with God and (3) One Holy Passion. A DPI best-seller. 3-cassette series.

Born Free

BY RYAN HOWARD

Three life-changing messages that will radically transform how you view who you are in Christ, how you can have confidence in your walk with God, and how to enjoy your life as a child of God. 3-cassette series.

Dating in the Kingdom

BY JIM AND TERESA BROWN

Two leaders in the New York City church who married after many years as successful, fruitful singles in the Kingdom present material on Christian dating that is Biblically rich, practically helpful and just plain fun! Not just for steady dating couples, this series contains a broad range of material covering the whole gamut of dating in the kingdom. 3-cassette series.